CREATIVE QUILT COLLECTION

VOLUME TWO

CREATIVE QUILT

From That Patchwork Place®

Martingale®
& COMPANY

COLLECTION

VOLUME TWO

Creative Quilt Collection Volume Two
© 2007 by Martingale & Company®

That Patchwork Place® is an imprint of Martingale & Company®.

Martingale & Company
20205 144th Ave. NE
Woodinville, WA 98072-8478 USA
www.martingale-pub.com

Printed in China
12 11 10 09 08 07   8 7 6 5 4 3 2 1

ISBN: 978-1-56477-773-7

MISSION STATEMENT

Dedicated to providing quality products and service to inspire creativity.

CREDITS

CEO: *Tom Wierzbicki*

Publisher: *Jane Hamada*

Editorial Director: *Mary V. Green*

Managing Editor: *Tina Cook*

Developmental Editor: *Karen Costello Soltys*

Technical Editor: *Laurie Baker*

Copy Editor: *Candie Frankel*

Design Director: *Stan Green*

Illustrators: *Laurel Strand and Robin Strobel*

Cover and Text Designer: *Trina Craig*

Photographer: *Brent Kane*

CONTENTS

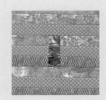

INTRODUCTION

THERE ARE SO many wonderful books to browse at the local quilt shop—as quilters, we wish we could bring them all home! What's the next best thing? This inspiring collection of quilt patterns from That Patchwork Place—18 specially selected designs from a bounty of our bestselling books. Here you can get a taste of all the best quilts from today's brightest designers.

Try TRADITION. From Sawtooth and Bear's Paw to Prairie Stars and Summer Winds, you'll find plenty of patterns steeped in tradition. If you're a beginning quilter, start with the simple project "Basket Weave" (page 43), a bed quilt in beautiful blue hues. The quilt "Idaho Farm Girl" (page 61) captures country charm in a classic two-block combination. For an heirloom quilt sure to become part of your Christmas tradition, stitch up "How Far Is It to Bethlehem?" (page 99), a gorgeous tribute to the story of the Nativity.

Try TRENDS. There's always a new trend to explore in quiltmaking, and here you'll find designs that are all the rage. "Spinners" (page 10) uses plaids, pinwheels, and a bounty of buttons in a fantastically fun throw. With folk art at the forefront of today's trends, the wall quilt "Late Summer Gatherings" (page 57) is perfect for complementing any primitive-style decor. And with "Blueberry Buckle" (page 69) and "A Bouquet of Stars" (page 92), you can plug in your favorite novelty fabric to make a quilt for any season—and any reason.

Try TECHNIQUES. If you want the exciting challenge of a new technique, look no further! Try the wildly popular Stack the Deck method in "Summer's End" (page 86). Take on curved piecing in sweet "Scrappy Circles Baby Quilt" (page 24). Appliqué the flower-filled wreaths in "Thinking of You" (page 38). Strip piece the simple quilt "The Amazon" (page 29) and get spectacular results. Or create the gorgeous quilt "Prairie Stars" (page 34) with shapes cut from strips.

Quick quilts for the wall, lap quilts for the couch, big quilts for the bed—turn to this pattern resource time and time again. Whether you want to make a quilt for everyday decor or special-occasion dazzle, you'll get a generous dose of inspiration in *Creative Quilt Collection Volume Two*. With the talents of so many topselling That Patchwork Place authors at your fingertips, you can unleash the cap on your creativity, starting today!

SPINNERS

From All Buttoned Up *by Loraine Manwaring and Susan Nelsen. Pieced and quilted by Loraine Manwaring.*

In the summertime, when tables are decked with brightly colored cloths and pinwheels appear in the backyard, you know it's time for a family picnic. Lively colors and plenty of pinwheels make this quilt the perfect complement to your outdoor decor.

Finished quilt size: 50" x 50"
Finished block size: 8" x 8"

MATERIALS

Yardage is based on 42"-wide fabric.

¼ yard *each* of 7 assorted prints for blocks
1 yard of yellow print for blocks
⅝ yard of green plaid for outer border
⅝ yard of blue print for blocks
½ yard of purple-and-green striped print for blocks
⅜ yard of multicolored dot print for inner border
⅓ yard of multicolored plaid for blocks and inner-border cornerstones
⅝ yard of red print for binding
3¼ yards of fabric for backing
56" x 56" piece of batting
25 assorted-color buttons, 1" diameter

CUTTING

All measurements include ¼"-wide seam allowances. Cut all strips across the width of the fabric.

From the yellow print, cut:
- 2 strips, 5¼" x 42"; crosscut into 13 squares, 5¼" x 5¼". Cut each square twice diagonally to yield 52 triangles.
- 4 strips, 4⅞" x 42"; crosscut into 26 squares, 4⅞" x 4⅞". Cut each square once diagonally to yield 52 triangles.

From *each* of the 7 assorted prints, cut:
- 1 strip, 5¼" x 42"; crosscut into 2 squares, 5¼" x 5¼". Cut each square twice diagonally to yield 8 triangles (56 *total*; 4 left over). From the remainder of 6 of the strips, cut 2 squares, 3¾" x 3¾"; cut each square twice diagonally to yield 8 triangles (48 *total*).

From the blue print, cut:
- 2 strips, 3¾" x 42"; crosscut into 12 squares, 3¾" x 3¾". Cut each square twice diagonally to yield 48 triangles.
- 3 strips, 3⅜" x 42"; crosscut into 24 squares, 3⅜" x 3⅜". Cut each square once diagonally to yield 48 triangles.

From the purple-and-green striped print, cut:
- 7 strips, 2" x 42"; crosscut into 48 pieces, 2" x 5½"

From the multicolored plaid, cut:
- 3 strips, 2" x 42"; crosscut into 48 squares, 2" x 2"
- 1 strip, 2½" x 42"; crosscut into 4 squares, 2½" x 2½"

From the multicolored dot print, cut:
- 4 strips, 2½" x 40½"

From the green plaid, cut:
- 5 strips, 3¼" x 42"

From the red print, cut:
- 6 strips, 2¾" x 42"

MAKING THE BLOCKS

Choose a different color for the pinwheel spinners of each block. The more variety you use, the scrappier your quilt will look.

1. To make block A, with right sides together, sew a yellow triangle cut from the 5¼" squares to each of four matching assorted-print triangles of the same size as shown to make triangle-square units. Press the seam allowances toward the assorted prints. Trim the dog-ears. *Note that the bias edges of the triangle-square units are on the outside; handle the pieces carefully to avoid stretching them.*

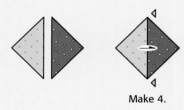

Make 4.

2. Join two triangle-square units as shown. Press the seam allowance as indicated. Make two.

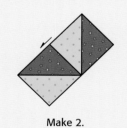

Make 2.

3. Sew the units together as shown. Before pressing, remove the vertical stitches in the seam allowances on both sides of each unit; then press the seam allowances in opposite directions. Where the eight points meet in the middle, press the seam allowances open so the unit makes a tiny pinwheel.

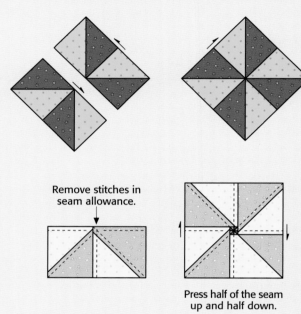

Remove stitches in seam allowance.

Press half of the seam up and half down.

4. Repeat steps 1–3 to make 13 spinner units *total*.

5. Sew a yellow triangle cut from the 4⅞" squares to opposite sides of each spinner unit. Press the seam allowances toward the corners. Sew a triangle to each of the remaining sides. Make 13 of block A.

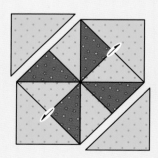
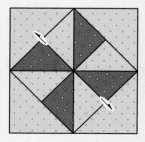

Block A.
Make 13.

6. To make block B, repeat step 1 with the blue print and assorted print triangles cut from the 3¾" squares.

Make 12
sets of 4.

7. Repeat steps 2 and 3 to join the units. Repeat step 5 to add the blue triangles cut from the 3⅜" squares to the sides.

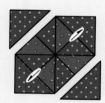

Make 12.

8. Sew a striped 2" x 5½" piece to opposite sides of each step 7 spinner unit as shown. Press the seam allowances toward the striped pieces.

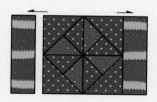

Make 12.

9. Sew a striped 2" x 5½" piece between two plaid 2" squares as shown. Press the seam allowances toward the striped pieces. Repeat to make 24 units *total*.

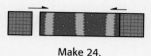

Make 24.

10. Sew the units from step 9 to the step 8 units as shown. Make 12 of block B.

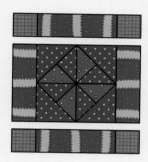 

Block B.
Make 12.

ASSEMBLING THE QUILT TOP

1. Arrange the blocks into five rows as shown on page 14, alternating the position of blocks A and B in each row and from row to row as shown. Sew the blocks in each row together, pressing the seam allowances in opposite directions from row to row. Join the rows. Press the seam allowances in one direction.

2. Referring to "Borders with Corner Squares" on page 115, sew a multicolored-dot 2½" x 40½" strip to the sides of the quilt for the inner border. Add the multicolored-plaid 2½" squares to the ends of the remaining two multicolored-dot strips. Sew these strips to the top and bottom of the quilt to complete the inner border.

Quilt assembly

3. Referring to "Borders with Butted Corners" on page 115, add the green plaid strips to the quilt for the outer border.

FINISHING THE QUILT

Refer to "Preparing to Quilt" on page 117, "Quilting Techniques" on page 118, and "Finishing Techniques" on page 119 for more detailed instructions, if needed.

1. Piece the quilt backing so that it is 4" to 6" longer and wider than the quilt top. Mark the quilt top if necessary. Layer the quilt top with batting and backing and baste the layers together—unless you plan to take your quilt to a long-arm quilter.

2. Hand or machine quilt as desired.

3. Trim the batting and backing even with the edges of the quilt top. Add a hanging sleeve if desired. Using the red 2¾"-wide strips, prepare the binding and sew it to the quilt.

4. Embellish your quilt by sewing the buttons in the centers of the spinners as shown in the photo on page 10.

5. Make a label and attach it to the back of the quilt.

SAWTOOTH MEDALLION

From A Treasury of Scrap Quilts *by Nancy J. Martin.*
Pieced and appliquéd by Mary Hickey. Quilted by
Fannie Schwartz.

Although this quilt makes good use of scraps, the color and placement of each fabric was carefully planned. Notice that a fabric from the same color family is used in the same position in each block.

Finished quilt size: 75" x 83"
Finished block size: 8" x 8"

MATERIALS

Yardage is based on 42"-wide fabric.

2⅝ yards of floral print for outer border
2⅜ yards *total* of assorted light pink prints for medallion background and blocks
2 yards *total* of assorted dark blue prints for blocks and appliqués
2 yards *total* of assorted medium blue prints for blocks and appliqués
¾ yard *total* of assorted medium pink prints for blocks
⅝ yard of light blue print for medallion background
⅝ yard of light pink print for inner border
⅜ yard of light blue print for medallion border
¼ yard *each* of 3 assorted green prints for appliqué
¼ yard *each* of 6 assorted rose prints for appliqué
1 yard of fabric for binding
5½ yards of fabric for backing
81" x 89" piece of batting
Bias Square® ruler to cut bias squares
½"-wide bias press bar for making stems

CUTTING

All measurements include ¼"-wide seam allowances. Cut all strips across the width of the fabric unless otherwise indicated.

From the assorted light pink prints for medallion background and blocks, cut:
- 2 squares, 10⅞" x 10⅞"; cut each square once diagonally to yield 4 large triangles

- 30 squares, 8" x 8"
- 47 squares, 2⅞" x 2⅞"; cut each square once diagonally to yield 94 small triangles

From the assorted dark blue prints, cut a *total* of:
- 30 squares, 8" x 8"

From the assorted medium pink prints, cut a *total* of:
- 24 squares, 4⅞" x 4⅞"; cut each square once diagonally to yield 48 triangles (1 left over)

From the assorted medium blue prints, cut a *total* of:
- 24 squares, 8⅞" x 8⅞"; cut each square once diagonally to yield 48 triangles (1 left over)

From the light blue print for medallion background, cut:
- 1 square, 14⅝" x 14⅝"

From the light blue print for medallion border, cut:
- 3 strips, 2½" x 42"

From the light pink print for inner border, cut:
- 7 strips, 2½" x 42"

From the *lengthwise grain* of the floral print, cut:
- 2 strips, 7¾" x 70"
- 2 strips, 7¾" x 77"

From the binding fabric, cut:
- 2¼"-wide bias strips to make a 325" length of binding

MAKING THE BLOCKS

1. Pair each light pink 8" square with a dark blue 8" square, right sides up. Cut the squares in half diagonally.

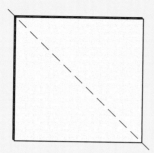

2. Using the first cut as a guide, cut 2½"-wide bias strips.

3. Separate and rearrange the strips in each pair, alternating the colors as shown. Sew the strips together along the bias edges, using a ¼" seam allowance. Be sure to align the strips so the lower edge and one adjacent edge form straight lines.

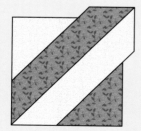

4. Starting at the lower-left corner, align the 45° mark of the Bias Square ruler on the seam line and the 2¾" lines with the side and bottom

edges. Cut along the side and bottom edges to release the square from the rest of the fabric.

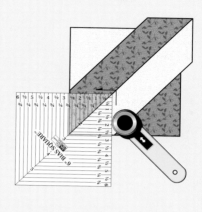

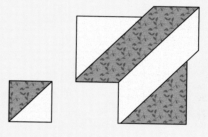

5. Turn the fabric square and place the Bias Square ruler on the opposite two uncut sides, aligning the 2½" ruler marks with the previously cut sides and the 45° mark with the seam. Cut the remaining two sides of the fabric square so that it measures 2½".

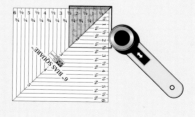

Turn segment and cut opposite 2 sides.

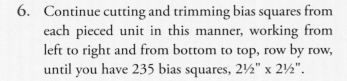

6. Continue cutting and trimming bias squares from each pieced unit in this manner, working from left to right and from bottom to top, row by row, until you have 235 bias squares, 2½" x 2½".

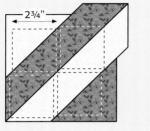

Cut 235.

7. Choosing fabrics randomly, join five bias squares, two small light pink triangles, and one medium pink triangle as shown to form a unit. Make 47.

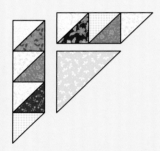
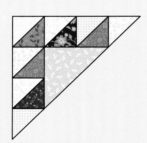

Make 47.

8. Stitch a medium blue triangle to each unit to make a Sawtooth block. Make 47.

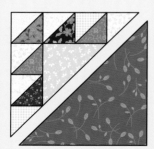
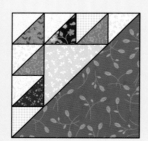

Make 47.

MAKING THE MEDALLION

1. Stitch the large light pink triangles to the sides of the light blue square, joining opposite sides first. Referring to "Borders with Butted Corners" on page 115, add the light blue 2½"-wide strips to the square for the medallion border.

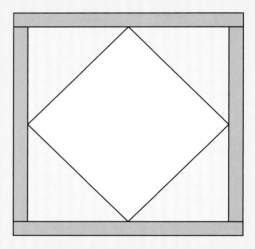

2. Referring to "Appliqué Basics" on page 111, choose an appliqué method and then use the patterns on pages 21–23 to cut out the appliqués from the appropriate fabrics, as indicated. Refer to "Making Bias Stems" on page 114 to cut the remainder of the green fabrics into 1¼"-wide bias strips and make bias tubes for the stems. Appliqué the pieces to the background as shown.

Appliqué placement

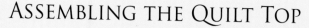

ASSEMBLING THE QUILT TOP

1. Arrange the blocks for rows 1 and 2 as shown, being careful to orient the blocks in the correct direction. Sew the blocks in each row together and then sew the rows together.

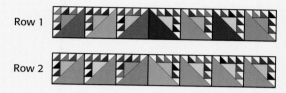

2. Arrange the blocks for the left side of rows 3, 4, and 5 as shown. Stitch the blocks together. Join the partial rows to the left side of the appliquéd medallion.

3. Arrange the blocks for the right side of rows 3, 4, and 5 as shown. Stitch the blocks in each row together and then stitch the rows together. Join the partial rows to the right side of the appliquéd medallion.

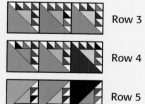

4. Arrange the blocks for rows 6, 7, and 8 as shown. Stitch the blocks in each row together and then stitch the rows together.

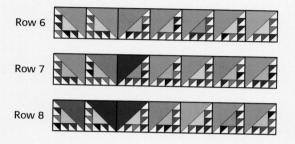

5. Join the sections of rows.

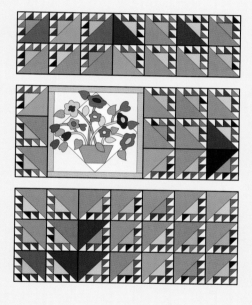

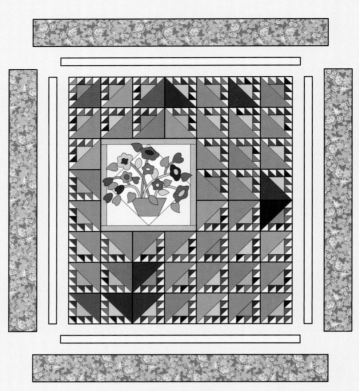

Quilt assembly

6. Referring to "Borders with Butted Corners" on page 115, sew the light pink 2½"-wide strips to the quilt top for the inner border. Measure the quilt for the outer border. Trim the floral 7¾"-wide strips to the exact lengths needed and attach them to the quilt top in the same manner as the inner border.

FINISHING THE QUILT

Refer to "Preparing to Quilt" on page 117, "Quilting Techniques" on page 118, and "Finishing Techniques" on page 119 for more detailed instructions, if needed.

1. Piece the quilt backing so that it is 4" to 6" longer and wider than the quilt top. Mark the quilt top if necessary. Layer the quilt top with batting and backing and baste the layers together—unless you plan to take your quilt to a long-arm quilter.

2. Hand or machine quilt as desired.

3. Trim the batting and backing even with the edges of the quilt top. Add a hanging sleeve if desired. Using the 2¼"-wide binding strips, prepare the binding and sew it to the quilt. Make a label and attach it to the back of the quilt.

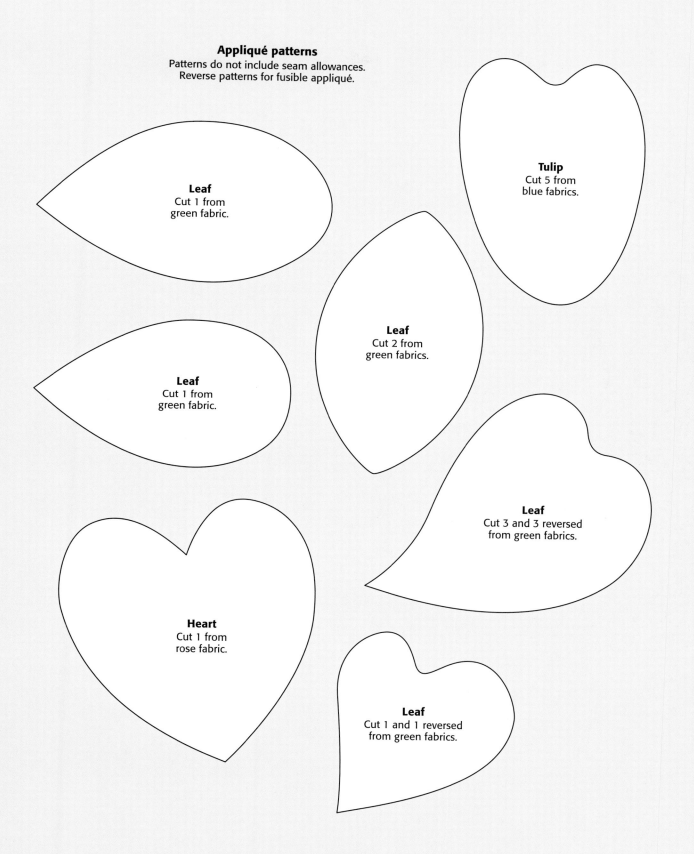

Appliqué patterns
Patterns do not include seam allowances.
Reverse patterns for fusible appliqué.

Leaf
Cut 1 from
green fabric.

Tulip
Cut 5 from
blue fabrics.

Leaf
Cut 2 from
green fabrics.

Leaf
Cut 1 from
green fabric.

Leaf
Cut 3 and 3 reversed
from green fabrics.

Heart
Cut 1 from
rose fabric.

Leaf
Cut 1 and 1 reversed
from green fabrics.

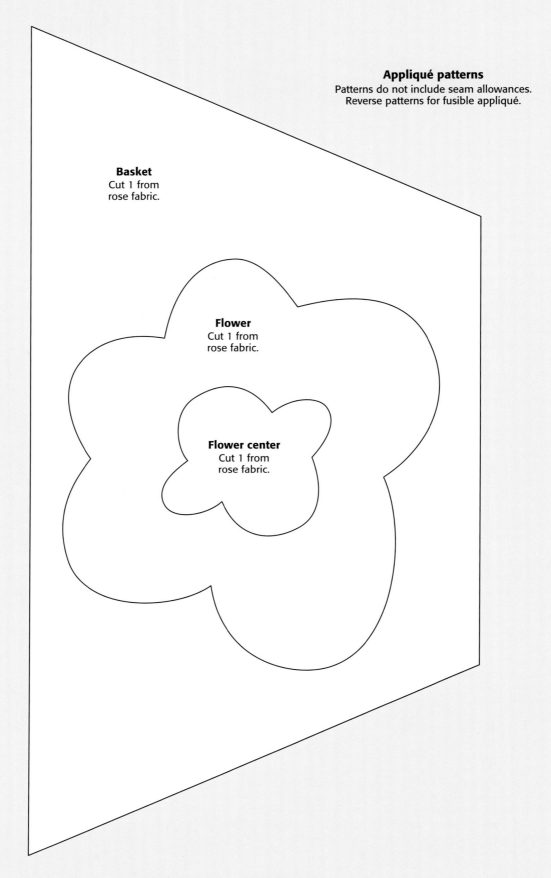

Appliqué patterns
Patterns do not include seam allowances.
Reverse patterns for fusible appliqué.

Basket
Cut 1 from
rose fabric.

Flower
Cut 1 from
rose fabric.

Flower center
Cut 1 from
rose fabric.

Appliqué patterns
Patterns do not include seam allowances.
Reverse patterns for fusible appliqué.

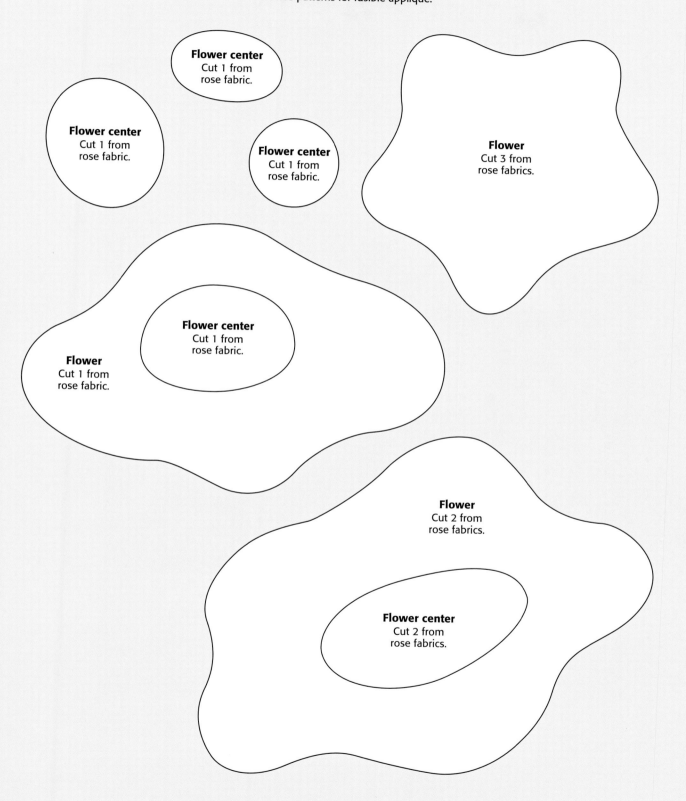

Flower center
Cut 1 from
rose fabric.

Flower center
Cut 1 from
rose fabric.

Flower center
Cut 1 from
rose fabric.

Flower
Cut 3 from
rose fabrics.

Flower center
Cut 1 from
rose fabric.

Flower
Cut 1 from
rose fabric.

Flower
Cut 2 from
rose fabrics.

Flower center
Cut 2 from
rose fabrics.

SCRAPPY CIRCLES BABY QUILT

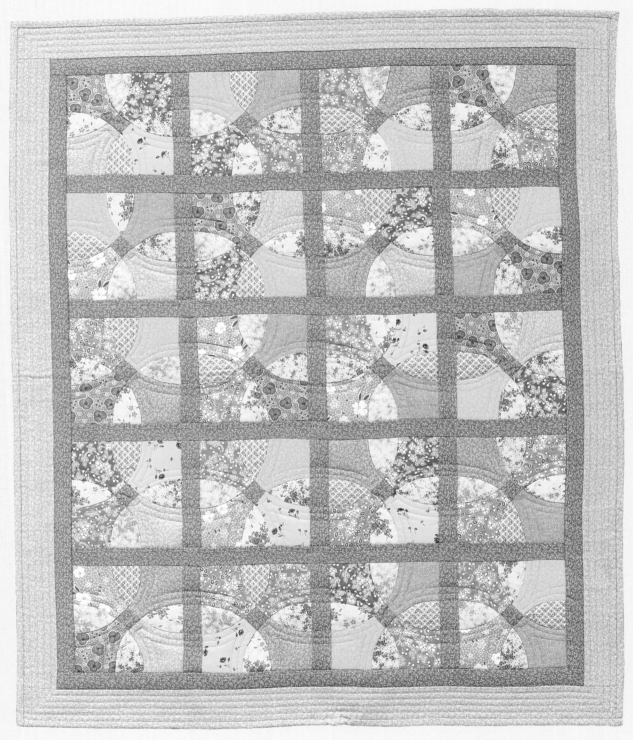

From The Blessed Home Quilt *by Myra Harder and Cori Derksen. Pieced by Myra Harder and Cori Derksen. Quilted by Myra Harder.*

Many people enjoy the look that curved pieces give to quilts, but they are too intimidated to try sewing the pieces. Sewing curves is really just as easy as sewing a straight line; it just takes a little more attention and a few more moments of preparation, but the results are worth it.

Finished quilt size: 33" x 40"
Finished block size: 6" x 6"

MATERIALS

Yardage is based on 42"-wide fabric.

⅛ yard *each* of 10 assorted medium prints for template A pieces

⅝ yard of dark pink print for template B pieces, sashing, and inner border

⅛ yard *each* of 4 assorted light prints for template C pieces

⅓ yard of medium print for outer border

⅜ yard of fabric for binding

1⅜ yards of fabric for backing

37" x 44" piece of batting

Template plastic

CUTTING

All measurements include ¼"-wide seam allowances. Cut all strips across the width of the fabric. For the cut shapes, read "Curved Piecing Basics" on page 26 and then use the A, B, and C patterns on page 28 to make templates from template plastic. Place each template on the right side of the appropriate fabric and use a sharp pencil to draw around it the number of times needed. Cut out the shapes with scissors.

From the dark pink print, cut:
- 11 strips, 1½" x 42"; crosscut 7 strips into:
    15 rectangles, 1½" x 6½"
    4 strips, 1½" x 27½"
    2 strips, 1½" x 29½"
    2 strips, 1½" x 34½"
- 20 template B pieces

From the 10 assorted medium prints, cut a *total* of:
- 80 template A pieces

From the 4 assorted light prints, cut a *total* of:
- 80 template C pieces

From the outer-border fabric, cut:
- 4 strips, 2½" x 42"

From the binding fabric, cut:
- 4 strips, 2½" x 42"

MAKING THE BLOCKS

Choose a different fabric for each A and C piece in the block.

1. Join one B piece and two A pieces as shown. Finger-press the seam allowances toward the A pieces. Make 20.

 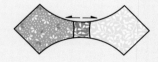

Make 20.

2. Sew a C piece to each curved side of an A piece as shown. Refer to "Curved Piecing Basics" on page 26. Finger-press the seam allowances toward the A piece. Make 40.

Make 40.

CURVED PIECING BASICS

MOST CURVED PIECES are cut with the aid of a template. We recommend using template plastic to make your template. Template plastic is easy to see through for tracing the pattern, is easy to cut, and will retain its shape over time. To make a template, simply trace the pattern for the shape onto template plastic using a fine-line permanent marker. Cut out the template on the outer line. The seam allowance has already been added to the patterns.

The most important rules in curved piecing are to mark the centers of the pieces and to use pins! Always mark the centers of the concave and convex pieces. To find the center, fold the piece in half along the curved edge. Crease the edge at the center or mark it with a pin or fabric marker. Lay the pieces on top of each other, right sides together, and then pin the pieces together at the centers and ends. Slowly sew from one end to the other using a ¼" seam allowance; gently ease the fabrics together. The curved edges are cut on the bias, which allow you to ease the two different curves to meet.

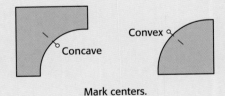

Mark centers.

Curved pieces can be easily distorted with an iron, so finger-press your seam allowances first, and then use your iron to press the finished block.

3. Pin a unit from step 2 to one curved edge of a unit from step 1, placing pins at the seam intersections and ends. Stitch the pieces together, gently easing in the fabric as you sew around the curve. Finger-press the seam toward the step 2 unit. Repeat to complete the block. Make 20. Use an iron to press the finished blocks.

 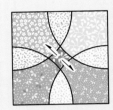

Make 20.

ASSEMBLING THE QUILT TOP

1. Join four blocks and three dark pink print 1½" x 6½" rectangles as shown to make a block row. Press the seam allowances toward the dark pink print strips. Make five rows.

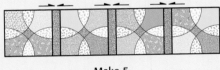

Make 5.

2. Sew the block rows and dark pink print 1½" x 27½" strips together as shown.

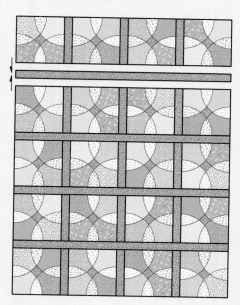

3. Refer to "Borders with Butted Corners" on page 115. For the inner border, sew the dark pink print 1½" x 34½" strips to the sides of the quilt top. Sew the dark pink print 1½" x 29½" strips to the top and bottom edges. Measure the quilt for the outer border and trim the outer-border strips as needed. Sew the outer-border fabric strips to the quilt top in the same manner as the inner border.

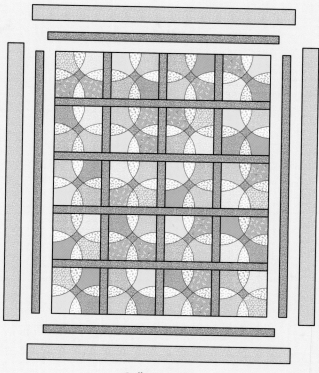

Quilt assembly

FINISHING THE QUILT

Refer to "Preparing to Quilt" on page 117, "Quilting Techniques" on page 118, and "Finishing Techniques" on page 119 for more detailed instructions, if needed.

1. Piece the quilt backing so that it is 4" to 6" longer and wider than the quilt top. Mark the quilt top if necessary. Layer the quilt top with batting and backing and baste the layers together—unless you plan to take your quilt to a long-arm quilter.

2. Hand or machine quilt as desired.

3. Trim the batting and backing even with the edges of the quilt top. Add a hanging sleeve if desired. Using the 2½"-wide binding strips, prepare the binding and sew it to the quilt. Make a label and attach it to the back of the quilt.

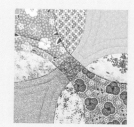

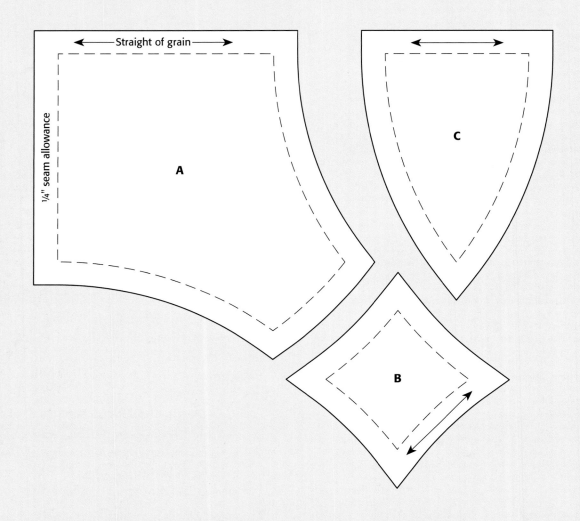

Straight of grain

¼" seam allowance

A

C

B

THE AMAZON

From Strip-Pieced Quilts *by Maaike Bakker.*
Made by Maaike Bakker and Els Oosterloo.

Blocks cut on the diagonal from a strip set made of blue and green fabrics transform this quilt into a rain forest crisscrossed by rivers.

Finished quilt size: 66¼" x 66¼"
Finished block size: 7" x 7"

MATERIALS

Yardage is based on 42"-wide fabric.

1 yard *each* of 6 colors ranging from light green to bluish
　green to purple for blocks and third border
2 yards of dark purple print for first and fourth borders
¼ yard of bright pink fabric for second border
¾ yard of variegated plaid for binding
4¼ yards of fabric for backing
74" x 74" piece of batting

CUTTING

All measurements include ¼"-wide seam allowances. Cut all strips across the width of the fabric.

From *each* of the 6 colors ranging from light green to purple, cut:

*   14 strips, 2" x 42" (84 *total*)

From the dark purple print, cut:

*   6 strips, 2" x 42"
*   8 strips, 6" x 42"

From the bright pink fabric, cut:

*   6 strips, ¾" x 42"

From the variegated plaid, cut:

*   3"-wide bias strips to make a 282" length of
    binding

MAKING THE BLOCKS

1. Arrange the six different light green to purple strips from light to dark. Sew the strips together along the long edges as shown to make a strip set. Press the seam allowances toward the darker colors. Make 14 strip sets.

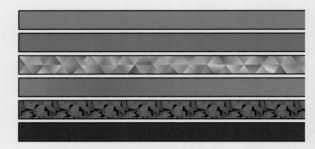

Arrange strips from light green to purple.

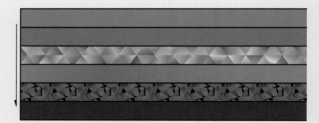

Make 14 strip sets.

2. Place a strip set on the cutting mat with the green strips closer to you. Straighten the right end of the strip. Mark a point along the top edge that is 2½" from the right end. Align the ruler with this mark and the lower-right corner. Cut along the edge of the ruler. Repeat with six additional strip sets (seven *total*).

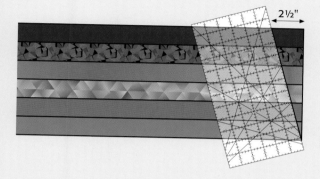

3. Rotate the cutting mat so that the cut end of one strip set from step 2 is on the left. Cut the strip set into four 7½" segments that are parallel to the first cutting line. Repeat with the remaining strip sets from step 2 to cut 28 segments *total*. Set aside the leftovers from each strip set.

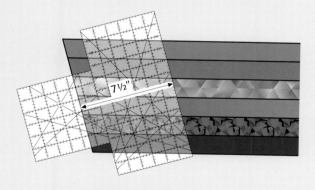

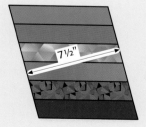

Cut 28.

4. From the remaining seven strip sets, cut 28 segments in reverse. Place a strip set on the cutting mat with the green strips closer to you. Straighten the right end. Mark a point along the bottom edge that is 2½" from the right end. Align the ruler with this mark and the upper-right corner. Cut along the edge of the ruler. Rotate the cutting mat so that the cut end of the strip set is on the left; cut four 7½" segments that are parallel to the first cutting line. Repeat with the remaining strip sets. Set aside the leftovers from each strip set.

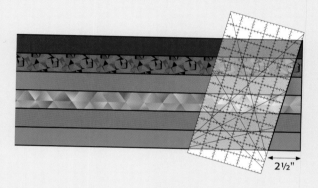

5. Cut the segments from steps 3 and 4 into 56 squares, 7½" x 7½", as shown, to make 28 of block A and 28 of block B.

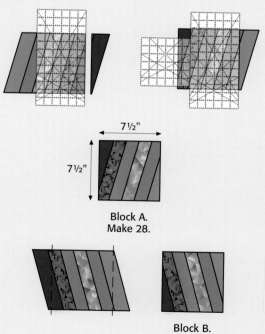

Block A.
Make 28.

Block B.
Make 28.

MAKING THE PIECED BORDER

1. Sew four A blocks and three B blocks together as shown.

2. Cut the row lengthwise into four strips, each 1⅞" wide.

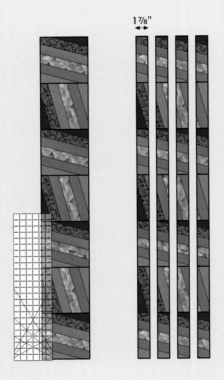

1⅞"

3. Cut four additional 1⅞"-wide segments from the strip-set leftovers as shown. Straighten the ends and sew one to each strip from step 2.

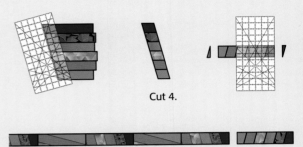

Cut 4.

4. Set the strips aside until you add the borders.

ASSEMBLING THE QUILT TOP

1. Arrange the remaining blocks into seven rows as shown, or play with the blocks on a design wall to determine a setting that you like. Sew the blocks into rows. Press the seam allowances in opposite directions from row to row. Join the rows. Press the seam allowances in one direction.

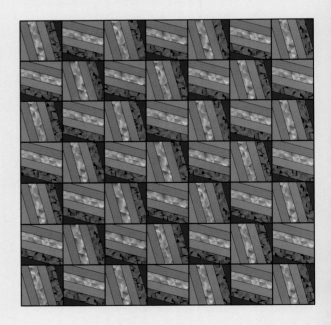

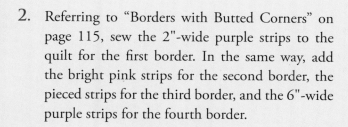

2. Referring to "Borders with Butted Corners" on page 115, sew the 2"-wide purple strips to the quilt for the first border. In the same way, add the bright pink strips for the second border, the pieced strips for the third border, and the 6"-wide purple strips for the fourth border.

FINISHING THE QUILT

Refer to "Preparing to Quilt" on page 117, "Quilting Techniques" on page 118, and "Finishing Techniques" on page 119 for more detailed instructions, if needed.

1. Piece the quilt backing so that it is 4" to 6" longer and wider than the quilt top. Mark the quilt top if necessary. Layer the quilt top with batting and backing and baste the layers together—unless you plan to take your quilt to a long-arm quilter.

2. Hand or machine quilt as desired.

3. Trim the batting and backing even with the edges of the quilt top. Slightly round the corners of the quilt, using a teacup or other round object. Add a hanging sleeve if desired. Using the 3"-wide bias binding strips, prepare the binding and sew it to the quilt. Make a label and attach it to the back of the quilt.

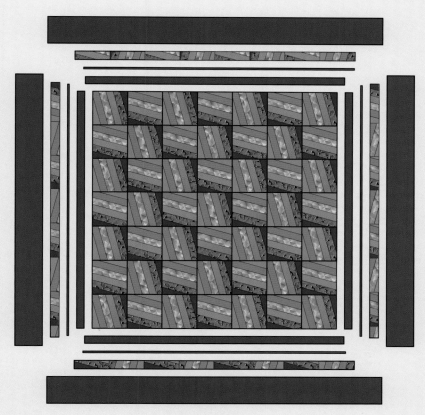

Quilt assembly

PRAIRIE STARS

From Twosey-Foursey Quilts
by Cathy Wierzbicki

Radiant stars in a constellation of colors light up any room in which you hang this quilt. Cathy's nifty All-in-One Ruler™ enables you to cut all of the shapes from strips.

Finished quilt size: 56½" x 56½"
Finished block size: 8" x 8"

MATERIALS

Yardage is based on 42"-wide fabric.

¼ yard *each* of 13 assorted dark fabrics for Star blocks and outer border

¼ yard *each* of 13 assorted light fabrics for Star blocks

1⅓ yards *total* of additional assorted light fabrics for alternate blocks and border blocks

¼ yard of red fabric for alternate blocks and border blocks

¼ yard of green fabric for alternate blocks and border blocks

½ yard of fabric for binding

3½ yards of fabric for backing

62" x 62" piece of batting

CUTTING

Measurements are given to cut the pieces using the All-in-One Ruler or the traditional equivalent. Pick whichever method you prefer. If you select the All-in-One Ruler method, follow the instructions given with the ruler to cut the pieces. All measurements include ¼"-wide seam allowances. Cut all strips across the width of the fabric.

In the Star blocks, pieces A and B form the star and pieces C and D make up the background. The A and B pieces for each star can be cut from the same fabric or you can cut the A piece from one fabric and the B pieces from a different fabric. However, both should contrast with the background pieces, which are all cut from the same fabric. In other words, if you use dark fabric(s) for pieces A and B, use a light fabric for pieces C and D.

Fabric	All-in-One Ruler	Traditional Equivalent
Assorted darks and lights	13 squares *total*, 4½" x 4½" (A)	13 squares *total*, 4½" x 4½" (A)
	13 strips *total*, 2½" x 14"; cut *each* strip into 8 half-square triangles (B)	13 sets of 4 squares, 2⅞"x 2⅞"; cut each square once diagonally to yield 8 half-square triangles (B)
	13 strips *total*, 2½" x 25"; cut *each* strip into: • 4 quarter-square triangles (C) • 4 squares (D)	13 squares *total*, 5¼"x 5¼"; cut each square twice diagonally to yield 52 quarter-square triangles (C)
		13 sets of 4 squares, 2½" x 2½" (D)
Additional assorted lights	9 strips *total*, 4½" x 42"; cut into: • 72 half-square triangles (E) • 20 squares, 4½" x 4½"	36 squares *total*, 4⅞"x 4⅞"; cut each square once diagonally to yield 72 half-square triangles (E)
		20 squares *total*, 4½" x 4½"
Green	2 strips, 2½" x 42"; cut into 40 half-square triangles (F)	2 strips, 2⅞" x 42"; crosscut into 20 squares, 2⅞" x 2⅞". Cut each square once diagonally to yield 40 half-square triangles (F).
Red	2 strips, 2½" x 42"; cut into 32 half-square triangles (F)	2 strips, 2⅞" x 42"; crosscut into 16 squares, 2⅞" x 2⅞". Cut each square once diagonally to yield 32 half-square triangles (F).
Binding	6 strips, 2½" x 42"	6 strips, 2½" x 42"

MAKING THE STAR BLOCKS

1. Sew matching B half-square triangles to the short sides of four matching C quarter-square triangles as shown.

Make 4.

2. Sew a unit from step 1 between two D squares that match the C triangles as shown. Press the seam allowances toward the squares. Make two.

Make 2.

3. Arrange and sew the units from steps 1 and 2 together with an A square as shown; press the seam allowances as indicated.

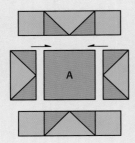 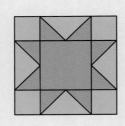

4. Repeat steps 1–3 to make 13 blocks *total*.

MAKING THE ALTERNATE BLOCKS

1. Sew a light E half-square triangle to each red and green F half-square triangle as shown. Press the seam allowances toward the red and green triangles.

Make 40.   Make 32.

2. Arrange two green units and two red units from step 1 into two rows as shown. Sew the units in each row together and then sew the rows together. Press the seam allowances as indicated. Make 12. You'll use the rest of the units for the border blocks.

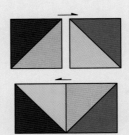 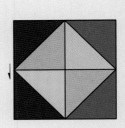

Make 12.

MAKING THE BORDER BLOCKS

1. Sew the remaining red half-square-triangle units into pairs as shown. Make four. Press the seam allowances as indicated.

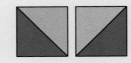 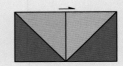

Make 4.

2. Repeat step 1 with the remaining green half-square-triangle units. Make eight.

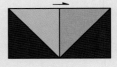

Make 8.

ASSEMBLING THE QUILT TOP

1. Arrange the Star and alternate blocks, the border blocks, and the light 4½" squares in six rows as shown in the quilt assembly diagram, positioning the alternate and border blocks so they form large secondary stars. Sew the blocks and squares

together into rows. Press the seam allowances as indicated. Sew the rows together. Press the seam allowances in one direction.

2. Cut the remaining dark fabric into 4½"-wide strips of random lengths. Sew the strips together to make two borders, 4½" x 48½", piecing them with diagonal seams. Sew these strips to the sides of the quilt. Press the seam allowances toward the border. Repeat to make two additional borders, 4½" x 56½", and sew them to the top and bottom of the quilt. Press the seam allowances toward the border. Be aware of the direction of the seams in the borders as you piece them together and add them to the quilt. All of the seams should run in the same direction when the borders are sewn to the quilt.

FINISHING THE QUILT

Refer to "Preparing to Quilt" on page 117, "Quilting Techniques" on page 118, and "Finishing Techniques" on page 119 for more detailed instructions, if needed.

1. Piece the quilt backing so that it is 4" to 6" longer and wider than the quilt top. Mark the quilt top if necessary. Layer the quilt top with batting and backing and baste the layers together—unless you plan to take your quilt to a long-arm quilter.

2. Hand or machine quilt as desired.

3. Trim the batting and backing even with the edges of the quilt top. Add a hanging sleeve if desired. Using the 2½"-wide binding strips, prepare the binding and sew it to the quilt. Make a label and attach it to the back of the quilt.

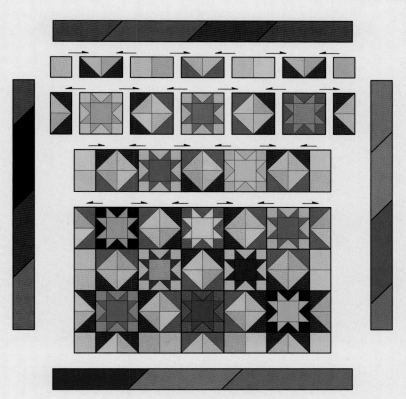

Quilt assembly

THINKING OF YOU

From Courtship Quilts *by Janna L. Sheppard*

The word pansy is actually a corruption of the French name for the flower, pensée, which also means "thought" or "thinking." This delightful little flower has had many charming and curious names through the ages. It's been called Cuddle-Me-to-You, Tittle My Fancy, Kiss Me at the Garden Gate, Love in Idleness, and Kiss Me Quick. At one time, it was believed that the pansy was the first flower pierced by Cupid's arrow. If you dream of this flower, it means "contentment."

Finished quilt size: 54½" x 54½"
Finished block size: 9" x 9"

MATERIALS

Yardage is based on 42"-wide fabric.

1⅜ yards of tan fabric for background of appliqué blocks and pieced blocks

⅞ yard of light gray fabric for outer border

⅞ yard *total* of assorted dark fabrics for pieced blocks

⅔ yard *total* of assorted light fabrics for pieced blocks

⅝ yard *total* of assorted green fabrics for bias stems and leaves

¼ yard of light red fabric for inner border

¼ yard of pink fabric for folded flange border

¼ yard *total* of assorted pink and red fabrics for flowers

½ yard of dark red fabric for binding

3½ yards of fabric for backing

61" x 61" piece of batting

½"-wide bias press bar for making stems

¼"-wide paper-backed fusible-web tape

Paper-backed fusible web

CUTTING

All measurements include ¼"-wide seam allowances. Cut all strips across the width of the fabric.

From the assorted dark fabrics, cut a *total* of:
- 16 strips, 1½" x 42"

From the assorted light fabrics, cut a *total* of:
- 14 strips, 1½" x 42"

From the tan fabric, cut:
- 4 squares, 9½" x 9½"
- 10 strips, 3½" x 42"; crosscut into:
    36 squares, 3½" x 3½"
    24 rectangles, 3½" x 9½"

From the pink fabric for folded flange border, cut:
- 5 strips, 1" x 42"

From the light red fabric, cut:
- 5 strips, 1" x 42"

From the light gray fabric, cut:
- 6 strips, 4½" x 42"

From the dark red fabric, cut:
- 6 strips, 2½" x 42"

MAKING THE BLOCKS

1. For strip set A, sew a dark 1½" x 42" strip to each long side of a light 1½" x 42" strip. Press the seam allowances toward the dark strips. Make six. From these strip sets, cut 141 segments, 1½" wide.

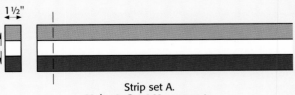

1½"

Strip set A.
Make 6. Cut 141 segments.

2. For strip set B, sew a light 1½" x 42" strip to each long side of a dark 1½" x 42" strip. Press the seam allowances toward the dark strip. Make four. From these strip sets, cut 102 segments, 1½" wide.

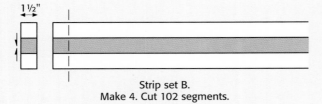

1½"

Strip set B.
Make 4. Cut 102 segments.

3. Sew one A segment to each side of a B segment to form a nine-patch unit. Make 60. In the same manner, sew a B segment to each side of an A segment. Make 21. Press the seam allowances as indicated.

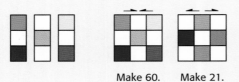

Make 60.   Make 21.

4. Select two nine-patch units with dark corners and one nine-patch unit with light corners. Sew them together as shown, being sure that the seams butt together in opposite directions. Press the seam allowances as indicated. Sew a 3½" x 9½" tan rectangle to each side of the nine-patch unit to make a Nine Patch Stripe block. Press the seam allowances toward the rectangles. Make 12.

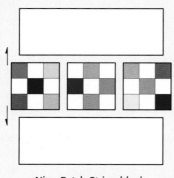

Nine Patch Stripe block.
Make 12.

5. Arrange four nine-patch units with dark corners, one nine-patch unit with light corners, and four tan 3½" squares together as shown. Sew the units into rows and then sew the rows together to complete the Double Nine Patch block. Press the seam allowances as indicated. Make nine.

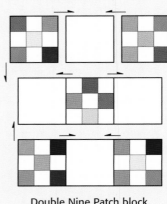

Double Nine Patch block.
Make 9.

ASSEMBLING THE QUILT TOP

1. Arrange the Double Nine Patch blocks, the Nine Patch Stripe blocks, and the tan 9½" squares as shown.

2. Sew the blocks and squares into rows and press the seam allowances toward the tan squares.

3. Sew the rows together and press the seam allowances toward the rows with tan squares.

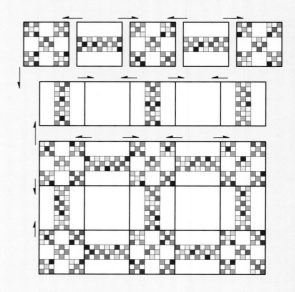

APPLIQUÉING THE PANSY WREATHS

1. To make the stems for the wreaths, refer to "Making Bias Stems" on page 114. Cut a *total* of four 1¼" x 27" bias strips from the assorted green fabrics and make bias stems.

2. Follow the manufacturer's instructions to center and fuse a length of fusible-web tape to the wrong side of each stem. Remove the paper backing.

3. Referring to the appliqué placement diagram, place the green bias stems on the tan squares to form the wreaths. Start and end at the bottom of each square so that the ends of the stems will be hidden under the large pansies. Fuse the stem in place. Hand or machine stitch the wreath in place using your preferred stitch.

4. Referring to "Fusible Appliqué" on page 113, trace the patterns on page 42 onto the paper side of the fusible web the amount of times indicated. Cut around the shapes and fuse them to the wrong sides of the appropriate fabrics, referring to the photo on page 38 as needed. Cut out the appliqué shapes on the marked lines. Remove the paper backing from the appliqué shapes. Referring to the placement diagram, arrange all of the flowers and leaves around the wreath circle and fuse them in place. Hand or machine stitch around each piece using your preferred stitch.

Appliqué placement

ADDING THE BORDERS

1. Sew the pink 1" x 42" strips together end to end. Press the seam allowances in one direction. Press the strip in half lengthwise, wrong sides together. From the pieced strip, cut four 45½" pieces. With raw edges even, pin a strip to the sides of the quilt, and then pin a strip to the top and bottom of the quilt, overlapping the ends at the corners.

2. Referring to "Borders with Butted Corners" on page 115, sew the light red strips to the quilt top for the inner border. The pink folded flange will be sandwiched between the red strips and the quilt top. Press the border seam allowances toward the border. Press the pink flange toward the quilt top. Measure the quilt top for the outer border. Sew the light gray strips to the quilt top in the same manner as the inner border.

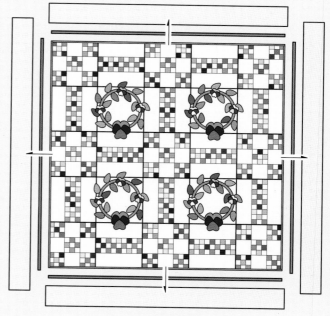

Quilt assembly

FINISHING THE QUILT

Refer to "Preparing to Quilt" on page 117, "Quilting Techniques" on page 118, and "Finishing Techniques" on page 119 for more detailed instructions, if needed.

1. Piece the quilt backing so that it is 4" to 6" longer and wider than the quilt top. Mark the quilt top if necessary. Layer the quilt top with batting and backing and baste the layers together—unless you plan to take your quilt to a long-arm quilter.

2. Hand or machine quilt as desired.

3. Trim the batting and backing even with the edges of the quilt top. Add a hanging sleeve if desired. Using the dark red 2½"-wide strips, prepare the binding and sew it to the quilt. Make a label and attach it to the back of the quilt.

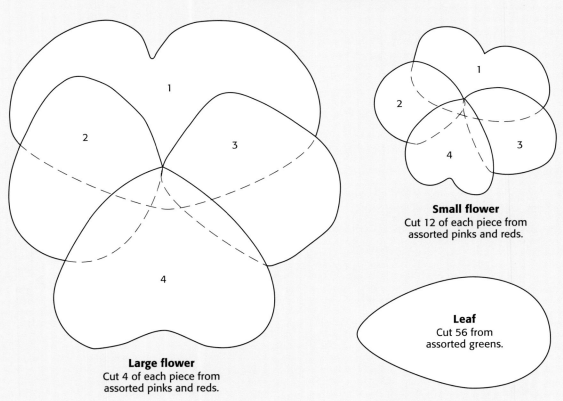

Appliqué patterns
Patterns do not include seam allowances.
Reverse patterns for fusible appliqué.

Large flower
Cut 4 of each piece from
assorted pinks and reds.

Small flower
Cut 12 of each piece from
assorted pinks and reds.

Leaf
Cut 56 from
assorted greens.

BASKET WEAVE

From Big 'n Easy *by Judy Hopkins. Pieced and quilted by Kathy White.*

Vertical pieces placed between strip-set segments make this quilt appear as if the strips were woven together like a basket. Choose fabrics that gradate from light to dark for added interest.

Finished quilt size: 96½" x 99"

MATERIALS

Yardage is based on 42"-wide fabric. You'll need anywhere from ⅓ yard to 1 yard of 13 assorted bluish green and blue prints for the horizontal strips as specified below. These fabrics should form a value gradation that runs from light aqua to dark blue, with fabric A being the lightest and fabric M being the darkest. Tape a snip of each of these fabrics to an index card and letter the snips for reference during the cutting and sewing process.

2⅛ yards of multicolored print for vertical bars and binding
⅓ yard *each* of fabrics A and M for horizontal strips
⅝ yard *each* of fabrics B and L for horizontal strips
1 yard *each* of fabrics C through K for horizontal strips
     (9 yards *total*)
9⅝ yards of fabric for backing*
103" x 105" piece of batting
Or combine fabric left over from making the front of the quilt with fabrics from your stash to make a pieced backing at least 103" x 105".

CUTTING

All measurements include ¼"-wide seam allowances. Cut all strips across the width of the fabric.

From *each* of fabrics A and M, cut:
- 5 strips, 2" x 42" (10 *total*)

From *each* of fabrics B and L, cut:
- 10 strips, 2" x 42" (20 *total*)

From *each* of fabrics C through K, cut:
- 15 strips, 2" x 42" (135 *total*)

From the multicolored print, cut:
- 8 strips, 5" x 42"; crosscut into 143 rectangles, 2" x 5"
- 11 strips, 2½" x 42"

MAKING THE ROWS

1. Join the 2" x 42" strips of fabrics A, B, and C as shown to make five strip sets. The lightest of the three fabrics should be at the top of the strip sets, and the darkest at the bottom. Press the seam allowances however you wish. From four of the strip sets, cut a total of 12 segments, 13" wide. From the fifth strip set, cut one segment, 13" wide, and two segments, 6" wide.

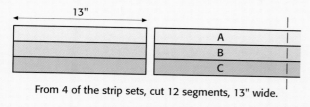

From 4 of the strip sets, cut 12 segments, 13" wide.

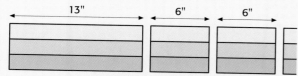

From the 5th strip set, cut 1 segment, 13" wide, and 2 segments, 6" wide.

2. Join the segments you cut in step 1 with 13 of the 2" x 5" multicolored print rectangles to make rows 1 and 2. Use seven 13" strip-set segments and six multicolored rectangles for row 1. Use six 13" strip-set segments, two 6" strip-set segments, and seven multicolored rectangles for row 2. Press the seam allowances however you wish.

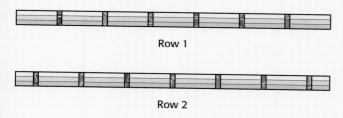

Row 1

Row 2

3. Repeat steps 1 and 2 using fabrics B, C, and D to make rows 3 and 4.

4. Repeat steps 1 and 2 using fabrics C, D, and E to make rows 5 and 6.

5. Repeat steps 1 and 2 using fabrics D, E, and F to make rows 7 and 8.

6. Repeat steps 1 and 2 using fabrics E, F, and G to make rows 9 and 10.

7. Repeat steps 1 and 2 using fabrics F, G, and H to make rows 11 and 12.

8. Repeat steps 1 and 2 using fabrics G, H, and I to make rows 13 and 14.

9. Repeat steps 1 and 2 using fabrics H, I, and J to make rows 15 and 16.

10. Repeat steps 1 and 2 using fabrics I, J, and K to make rows 17 and 18.

11. Repeat steps 1 and 2 using fabrics J, K, and L to make rows 19 and 20.

12. Repeat steps 1 and 2 using fabrics K, L, and M to make rows 21 and 22.

Assembling the Quilt Top

Join the rows as shown, aligning the multicolored print rectangles in the even rows and the multicolored print rectangles in the odd rows. Press the seam allowances however you wish.

Finishing the Quilt

Refer to "Preparing to Quilt" on page 117, "Quilting Techniques" on page 118, and "Finishing Techniques" on page 119 for more detailed instructions, if needed.

1. Piece the quilt backing so that it is 4" to 6" longer and wider than the quilt top. Mark the quilt top if necessary. Layer the quilt top with batting and backing and baste the layers together—unless you plan to take your quilt to a long-arm quilter.

2. Hand or machine quilt as desired.

3. Trim the batting and backing even with the edges of the quilt top. Add a hanging sleeve if desired. Using the multicolored print 2½"-wide strips, prepare the binding and sew it to the quilt. Make a label and attach it to the back of the quilt.

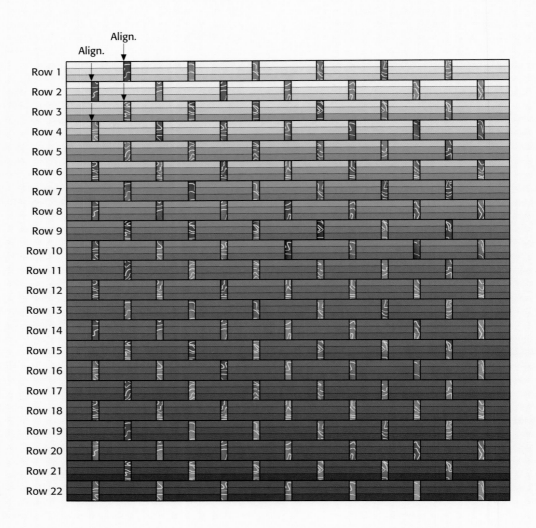

EVOLUTION

From Quilting Through Life *by Julia Teters-Ziegler. Pieced and hand appliquéd by Linda Jackson. Quilted by Jeri Lindstrom.*

This pattern offers a little bit of everything: piecing, appliqué, and a great opportunity to showcase your favorite large-scale floral fabric.

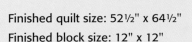

Finished quilt size: 52½" x 64½"
Finished block size: 12" x 12"

MATERIALS

Yardage is based on 42"-wide fabric.

3 yards of large-scale floral for blocks and outer border

1⅝ yards of apricot solid for blocks and inner border

1¼ yards of plum small-scale floral for appliqués and binding

⅝ yard of plum solid for blocks

3⅛ yards of fabric for backing

56" x 68" piece of batting

CUTTING

All measurements include ¼"-wide seam allowances. Cut all strips across the width of the fabric unless otherwise indicated.

From the *lengthwise grain* of the apricot solid, cut:
• 4 strips, 2½" x 50"

From the remaining apricot solid, cut:
• 48 squares, 3½" x 3½"
• 48 squares, 1½" x 1½"

From the plum solid, cut:
• 5 strips, 3½" x 42"; crosscut into 48 squares, 3½" x 3½"

From the *lengthwise grain* of the large-scale floral, cut:
• 4 strips, 6½" x 55"

From the remaining large-scale floral, cut:
• 48 squares, 6½" x 6½"

MAKING THE BLOCKS

1. Draw a diagonal line on the wrong side of each apricot 3½" square and each plum 3½" square. Align a marked apricot square right sides together with the upper-right corner of one 6½" large-scale floral square and stitch on the marked line. Trim ¼" from the stitched line as shown. Press the seam open. Repeat to sew a 3½" plum square to the lower-left corner of each unit as shown. Trim and press. Make 48.

Make 48.

2. Repeat step 1 to stitch a 1½" apricot square to the bottom-left corner of each unit from step 1. Make 48.

Make 48.

3. Arrange four units from step 2, taking care to turn the units as shown. Stitch the units into rows; press the seam allowances as indicated. Sew the rows together; press the seam allowances toward the bottom of the blocks. Make 12. Referring to "Squaring Up Blocks" on page 114, trim the blocks to 12½" x 12½".

Make 12.

4. Referring to "Appliqué Basics" on page 111, choose an appliqué method and then use the pattern on page 50 to cut out 48 petal appliqués from the plum small-scale floral. Appliqué four petals to each block so they meet in the center of the block as shown.

ASSEMBLING THE QUILT TOP

1. Refer to the quilt assembly diagram to arrange the blocks in four rows of three blocks each. Sew the blocks into rows; press the seam allowances in opposite directions from row to row. Sew the rows together; press the seam allowances in one direction.

2. Referring to "Borders with Butted Corners" on page 115, measure the quilt top for the inner border. Trim the apricot strips to the length needed and sew them to the quilt top. Measure the quilt for the outer border. Trim the large-scale floral strips to the length needed and sew them to the quilt top in the same manner as the inner border.

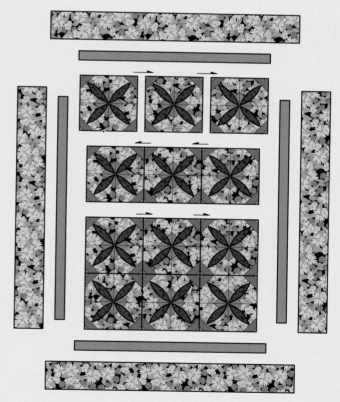

Quilt assembly

FINISHING THE QUILT

Refer to "Preparing to Quilt" on page 117, "Quilting Techniques" on page 118, and "Finishing Techniques" on page 119 for more detailed instructions, if needed.

1. Piece the quilt backing so that it is 4" to 6" longer and wider than the quilt top. Mark the quilt top if necessary. Layer the quilt top with batting and backing and baste the layers together—unless you plan to take your quilt to a long-arm quilter.

2. Hand or machine quilt as desired.

3. Trim the batting and backing even with the edges of the quilt top. Add a hanging sleeve if desired. From the remaining plum small-scale floral, cut enough 2½"-wide bias strips to make a 246" length of binding. Prepare the binding and sew it to the quilt. Make a label and attach it to the back of the quilt.

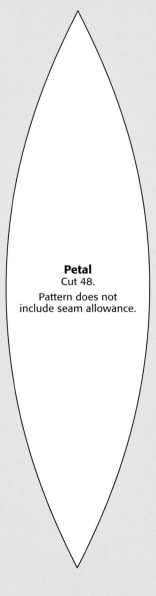

Petal
Cut 48.
Pattern does not
include seam allowance.

ARIZONA WINDS

From Two-Block Theme Quilts *by Claudia Olson.*
Designed by Claudia Olson, pieced by Pat Peyton,
and machine quilted by Jill Therriault.

In this two-block setting, a lovely fairy print fills the center of the Arizona blocks, while the Summer Winds blocks feature pastel colors that create a soft, unifying background. For your focus fabric, choose a print with motifs that will fit in a 4" x 5" rectangle.

Finished quilt size: 72½" x 72½"
Finished block size: 12" x 12"

MATERIALS

Yardage is based on 42"-wide fabric.

2 yards of lavender floral for Summer Winds blocks, border, and binding

1⅝ yards of rose print for blocks

1⅛ yards of pink print for blocks and pieced inner border

1⅛ yards of cream print for blocks and pieced inner border

1 yard of yellow print for blocks and pieced inner border

⅞ yard of light green print for blocks and pieced inner border

⅝ yard of purple print for blocks

⅝ yard of focus fabric for Arizona blocks*

4½ yards of fabric for backing

79" x 79" piece of batting

Extra fabric has been added for fussy cutting. Purchase this amount, or enough for 13 character repeats.

CUTTING

All measurements include ¼"-wide seam allowances. Cut all strips across the width of the fabric.

From the cream print, cut:
- 9 strips, 2⅞" x 42"; crosscut into 112 squares, 2⅞" x 2⅞"
- 1 strip, 2½" x 42"; crosscut into 16 squares, 2½" x 2½"
- 1 strip, 4½" x 42"; crosscut into 12 rectangles, 2½" x 4½"

From the rose print, cut:
- 8 strips, 2⅞" x 42"; crosscut into 104 squares, 2⅞" x 2⅞"

- 3 strips, 4½" x 42"; crosscut into:
  26 rectangles, 2½" x 4½"
  26 rectangles, 2" x 4½"
- 3 strips, 2½" x 42"; crosscut into 48 squares, 2½" x 2½"

From the pink print, cut:
- 4 strips, 2⅞" x 42"; crosscut into 46 squares, 2⅞" x 2⅞"
- 2 strips, 5¼" x 42"; crosscut into 12 squares, 5¼" x 5¼"
- 5 strips, 2½" x 42"; crosscut into 72 squares, 2½" x 2½"

From the purple print, cut:
- 6 strips, 2⅞" x 42"; crosscut into 74 squares, 2⅞" x 2⅞"

From the yellow print, cut:
- 3 strips, 5¼" x 42"; crosscut into 15 squares, 5¼" x 5¼"
- 3 strips, 4½" x 42"; crosscut into 48 rectangles, 2½" x 4½"

From the focus fabric, fussy cut:
- 13 rectangles, 4½" x 5½"

From the light green print, cut:
- 4 strips, 2⅞" x 42"; crosscut into 48 squares, 2⅞" x 2⅞"
- 5 strips, 2½" x 42"; crosscut into 72 squares, 2½" x 2½"

From the lavender floral, cut:
- 10 strips, 4½" x 42"; crosscut 2 strips into 12 squares, 4½" x 4½"
- 8 strips, 2¼" x 42"

MAKING THE ARIZONA BLOCKS

1. Referring to "Triangle Squares" on page 109, layer 52 cream 2⅞" squares on 52 rose 2⅞" squares. Mark, stitch, cut, and press to make 104 triangle squares. Repeat with 26 pink and purple 2⅞" squares to make 52 triangle squares.

Make 104.   Make 52.

2. Sew a cream-and-rose triangle square to a light green 2½" square as shown. Then sew a cream-and-rose triangle square to a pink-and-purple triangle square as shown. Make 52 of each. Press the seam allowances as indicated. Sew the units together to make a four-patch unit. Make 52. Press the seam allowances as indicated.

Make 52.

3. Referring to "Flying-Geese Units" on page 110, position two rose 2⅞" squares on opposite corners of a yellow 5¼" square. Mark, stitch, cut, and press. Make 13. Position a rose 2⅞" square on the remaining yellow corners. Stitch, cut, and press to make 52 flying-geese units.

Make 52.

4. Sew a flying-geese unit to a rose 2½" x 4½" rectangle as shown. Then sew a flying-geese unit to a rose 2" x 4½" rectangle. Make 26 of each. Press the seam allowances toward the rectangles.

Make 26 of each.

5. Lay out the pieced units along with a focus fabric 4½" x 5½" rectangle in vertical rows as shown. Sew the units together in each row. Press the seam allowances as indicated. Join the rows to complete the Arizona block. Make 13. Press the seam allowances as indicated.

Make 13.

MAKING
THE SUMMER WINDS BLOCKS

1. Referring to "Triangle Squares" on page 109, layer 48 cream 2⅞" squares on 48 purple 2⅞" squares. Mark, stitch, cut, and press to make 96 triangle squares.

Make 96.

2. Sew a triangle square to a pink 2½" square as shown. Then sew a rose 2½" square to a triangle square as shown. Make 48 of each. Press the seam allowances as indicated. Sew the units together to make a four-patch unit. Make 48. Press the seam allowances as indicated.

Make 48.

3. Referring to "Flying-Geese Units" on page 110, place two light green 2⅞" squares on opposite corners of a pink 5¼" square. Mark, stitch, cut, and press. Make 12. Place green 2⅞" squares on the remaining pink corners. Stitch, cut, and press to make 48 flying-geese units.

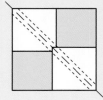

Make 48.

4. Sew yellow 2½" x 4½" rectangles to the flying-geese units. Make 48. Press the seam allowances toward the rectangles.

Make 48.

5. Lay out the pieced units and the lavender floral 4½" squares in vertical rows as shown. Sew the units together in each row. Press the seam allowances as indicated. Join the rows to complete a Summer Winds block. Make 12. Press the seam allowances as indicated.

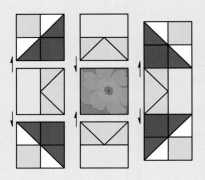

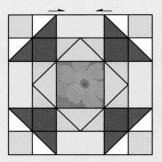

Make 12.

MAKING THE PIECED BORDER

1. Referring to "Triangle Squares" on page 109, layer 12 cream 2⅞" squares on 12 pink 2⅞" squares. Mark, stitch, cut, and press to make 24 triangle squares.

Make 24.

2. Sew the triangle squares to opposite ends of a cream 2½" x 4½" rectangle. Make 12. Press the seam allowances toward the rectangles.

Make 12.

3. Sew a pink 2½" square to each end of the unit made in step 2 to make a section 1 unit. Make 12. Press the seam allowances toward the squares.

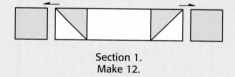

Section 1.
Make 12.

4. Referring to "Flying-Geese Units" on page 110, position two pink 2⅞" squares on a yellow 5¼" square. Mark, stitch, cut, and press. Make two. Place pink 2⅞" squares on the remaining yellow corners. Stitch, cut, and press to make eight flying-geese units.

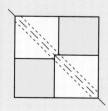

Make 8.

5. Sew a cream 2½" square and a light green 2½" square to both ends of the flying-geese units as shown to make a section 2 unit. Make eight.

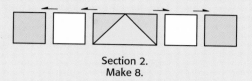

Section 2.
Make 8.

6. Sew three section 1 units and two section 2 units together, alternating them as shown to make a pieced border. Make four. Sew a light green 2½" square to both ends of two of the pieced borders.

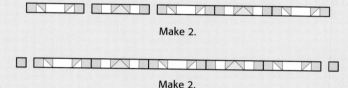

Make 2.

Make 2.

ASSEMBLING THE QUILT TOP

1. Arrange the blocks in five rows of five blocks each, alternating the blocks as shown on page 56. Sew the blocks into rows; press the seam allowances in opposite directions from row to row. Sew the rows together; press the seam allowances in one direction.

2. Sew the two pieced borders without green squares to opposite sides of the quilt top.

3. Sew the two borders with green squares to the top and bottom edges of the quilt.

4. Referring to "Borders with Mitered Corners" on page 116, make four lavender floral border strips that measure 4½" x 75". Match centers, pin, and sew the border strips to all four sides of the quilt top. Miter the corners.

Quilt assembly

FINISHING THE QUILT

Refer to "Preparing to Quilt" on page 117, "Quilting Techniques" on page 118, and "Finishing Techniques" on page 119 for more detailed instructions, if needed.

1. Piece the quilt backing so that it is 4" to 6" longer and wider than the quilt top. Mark the quilt top if necessary. Layer the quilt top with batting and backing and baste the layers together—unless you plan to take your quilt to a long-arm quilter.

2. Hand or machine quilt as desired.

3. Trim the batting and backing even with the edges of the quilt top. Add a hanging sleeve if desired. Using the lavender floral 2¼"-wide strips, prepare the binding and sew it to the quilt. Make a label and attach it to the back of the quilt.

LATE SUMMER GATHERINGS

From Primitive Gatherings *by Terry Burkhart and Rozan Meacham. Hand appliquéd and machine quilted by Rozan Meacham.*

It's late summer and fall is just around the corner. The sunflowers are shining their golden faces and the purple coneflowers are displaying their last glorious blooms. Rozan arranged a gathering of these last beautiful blossoms in an old sap bucket that her daughters brought from New England. Then she placed them on the dining-room table and added one of her beloved stuffed crows. This still life arrangement inspired the captivating wall hanging you see here.

Finished quilt size: 22" x 25"

MATERIALS

Yardage is based on 42"-wide fabric.

¾ yard of black-and-tan check for background and binding

1 fat quarter *each* of medium green print and dark green solid for leaves and stems

⅜ yard of brown print for outer border

⅜ yard of black fabric for inner border and crow body

1 fat quarter of red print for sap bucket and handle

1 fat eighth *each* of light gold print and dark gold print for sunflower petals and crow beak

5" x 5" piece *each* of light purple print and medium purple print for coneflowers

5" x 5" piece of gold print for star

5" x 5" piece of black fabric with dots for sunflower center

Scrap of brown print for coneflower cones

Scrap of black print for crow wing

¾ yard of fabric for backing

26" x 29" piece of lightweight cotton batting

Freezer paper

Chalk pencil

Size 10 appliqué needle or straw needle

Threads to match appliqué fabrics

Yellow thread

Roxanne's Glue-Baste-It

CUTTING

All measurements include ¼"-wide seam allowances. Note that the black-and-tan background piece is cut oversize to allow for some shrinkage from the appliqué and will be cut to size later.

From the black-and-tan check, cut:
- 1 piece, 16" x 19"
- 2¼"-wide bias strips to make a 115" length of binding

From the black fabric, cut:
- 2 strips, 1½" x 18"
- 2 strips, 1½" x 17"

From the brown print for outer border, cut:
- 2 strips, 3" x 20"
- 2 strips, 3" x 22"

APPLIQUÉING THE DESIGN

1. Referring to "Freezer-Paper Appliqué" on page 112, enlarge the patterns on page 60 and make freezer-paper templates for the appliqué shapes. Referring to the photo on page 57 and the materials list, iron the shapes onto the right side of the appropriate fabrics and trace around them using a chalk pencil. Cut them out, adding a ¼" seam allowance. Remove the freezer-paper templates.

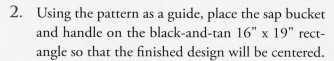

2. Using the pattern as a guide, place the sap bucket and handle on the black-and-tan 16" x 19" rectangle so that the finished design will be centered.

3. Add the two stems for the coneflowers—the longer stem under the handle and the shorter stem over the handle. A dotted line on the pattern means that part of the appliqué is under another appliqué.

4. Add the two coneflower, petals, the cones, and the coneflower leaves.

5. Add the sunflower leaf, sunflower petals, and sunflower center.

6. Add the crow body, crow beak, crow wing, and star.

7. Using Roxanne's Glue-Baste-It, add little dots of glue behind each piece. Referring to "Needle-Turn Appliqué" on page 111, appliqué each piece in place with matching thread. (If you prefer, you can position and appliqué the pieces one at a time.)

8. To make the crow's eye, use yellow thread and sew two straight stitches to make a plus sign (+). Then add two more lines to make an X over the plus sign.

9. After the appliqué is complete, trim the background piece to 15" x 18".

ASSEMBLING THE QUILT TOP

1. Sew the black 1½" x 18" strips to the sides of the appliquéd rectangle. Press the seam allowances toward the strips. Sew the 1½" x 17" strips to the top and bottom. Press the seam allowances toward the strips.

2. Sew the 3" x 20" brown print strips to the sides of the quilt. Sew the 3" x 22" brown print strips to the top and bottom of the quilt.

FINISHING THE QUILT

Refer to "Preparing to Quilt" on page 117, "Quilting Techniques" on page 118, and "Finishing Techniques" on page 119 for more detailed instructions, if needed.

1. Piece the quilt backing so that it is 4" to 6" longer and wider than the quilt top. Mark the quilt top if necessary. Layer the quilt top with batting and backing and baste the layers together.

2. Hand or machine quilt as desired.

3. Use a chalk marking pencil to randomly mark scallops around the outside of the brown print border. The scallops are random and not meant to be perfect or symmetrical. Use a rotary cutter to trim along the scalloped edges. Add a hanging sleeve if desired. Using the black-and-tan bias strips, prepare the binding and sew it to the quilt. Make a label and attach it to the back of the quilt.

Appliqué patterns
Enlarge patterns 167%.
Cut 1 of each piece.

Patterns do not include seam allowances.
Reverse patterns for fusible appliqué.

Embroidery placement

IDAHO FARM GIRL

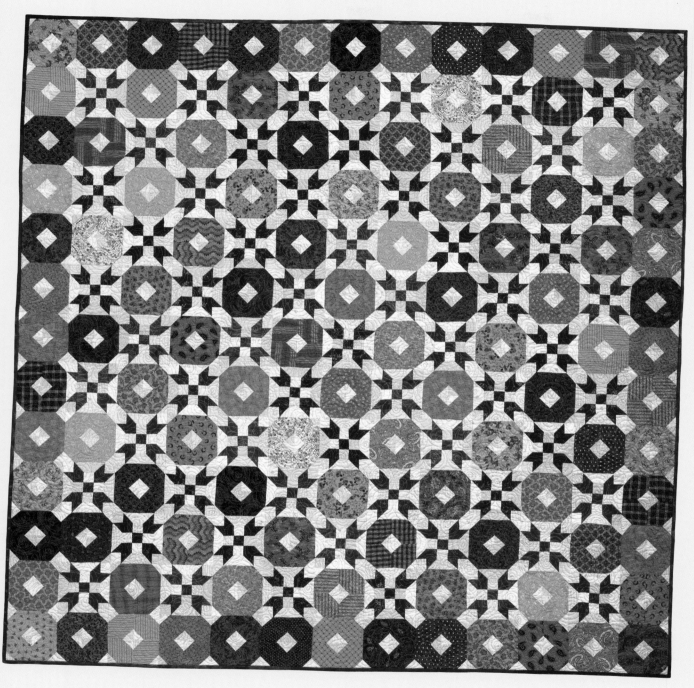

From Simple Traditions *by Kim Diehl. Designed
by Kim Diehl, machine pieced by Evelyne Schow,
and machine quilted by Kathy Ockerman.*

Awash with color and soft as a gentle rain, this quilt blooms with all the modest charm of a farmhouse garden. Wrap yourself in warmth and sit a spell as the virtues of country living soothe your soul.

Finished quilt size: 65½" x 65½"
Finished block size: 5" x 5"

MATERIALS

Yardage is based on 42"-wide fabric.

3½ yards *total* of assorted cream prints for block backgrounds

3⅛ yards *total* of assorted light, medium, and dark prints for blocks

2 yards *total* of assorted red prints for blocks and binding

4 yards of fabric for backing

72" x 72" piece of batting

CUTTING

All measurements include ¼"-wide seam allowances. Cut all strips across the width of the fabric.

From the assorted cream prints, cut a *total* of:
• 1,352 squares, 1½" x 1½"
• 244 rectangles, 1½" x 3½"

From the assorted light, medium, and dark prints, cut a *total* of:
• 432 squares, 3" x 3", in matching sets of 4

From the assorted red prints, cut a *total* of:
• 793 squares, 1½" x 1½", in matching sets of 13

From the remainder of the assorted red prints, cut:
• 2½"-wide random-length strips to make a 272" length of binding

MAKING THE SNOWBALL VARIATION BLOCKS

1. Draw a diagonal line on the wrong side of 864 assorted cream print 1½" squares.

2. Select one set of four matching light, medium, or dark 3" squares. With right sides together, position a marked cream square on one corner of each 3" square in the set as shown. Referring to "Chain Piecing" on page 109, stitch each layered pair together exactly on the drawn line.

Make 4.

3. Repeat step 2, placing a marked cream square on the opposite corner of each 3" square.

Make 4.

4. Press the half of the cream square that is closest to the center of the larger square over its opposite half, aligning the edges with the corner of the larger square. Trim away the excess layers of fabric under the top triangle, leaving a ¼" seam allowance.

Make 4.

5. Lay out the pieced units in two rows of two units each as shown. Join the units in each row. Press the seam allowances in opposite directions. Join the block halves. Press the seam allowances open.

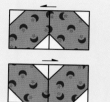 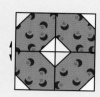

6. Repeat steps 2–5 using the remaining sets of light, medium, and dark print 3" squares to make 108 Snowball Variation blocks *total*. The blocks should measure 5½" square.

MAKING THE FARMER'S DAUGHTER BLOCKS

1. Select one set of 13 matching red print 1½" squares. Lay out five red print squares and four cream 1½" squares in three rows as shown to form a nine-patch unit. Join the pieces in each row. Press the seam allowances toward the red squares. Join the rows. Press the seam allowances away from the center row.

2. Draw a diagonal line on the wrong side of the eight remaining red print squares from the set.

3. With right sides together, align a marked red print square on opposite ends of a cream print 1½" x 3½" rectangle as shown, placing them in mirror-image positions. Sew the layers together exactly on the drawn lines. Press and trim as instructed for the Snowball Variation blocks. Repeat to make four units *total*.

Make 4.

4. Arrange the units from step 3, four cream print 1½" squares, and the nine-patch unit into three rows as shown. Sew the units in each row together. Press the seam allowances as indicated. Join the rows to complete a Farmer's Daughter block. Press the seam allowances as indicated.

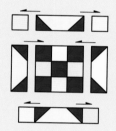 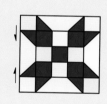

5. Repeat steps 1–4 to make 61 Farmer's Daughter blocks. The blocks should measure 5½" square.

ASSEMBLING THE QUILT TOP

1. Lay out 13 Snowball Variation blocks as shown to make row A. Join the blocks. Press the seam allowances all in one direction. Repeat to make two A rows.

Row A.
Make 2.

2. Lay out seven Snowball Variation blocks and six Farmer's Daughter blocks in alternating positions as shown to make row B. Join the blocks. Press the seam allowances toward the Snowball Variation blocks. Repeat to make six B rows.

Row B.
Make 6.

3. Lay out eight Snowball Variation blocks and five Farmer's Daughter blocks as shown to make row C. Join the blocks. Press the seam allowances of the first and last Snowball Variation blocks toward the center of the row. Press the remaining seam allowances toward the Snowball Variation blocks. Repeat to make five C rows.

Row C.
Make 5.

4. Refer to the quilt assembly diagram to lay out the B rows and C rows, alternating positions. Sew the rows together. Press the seam allowances open.

5. Join a row A to the top and bottom of the quilt top. Press the seam allowances toward the A rows.

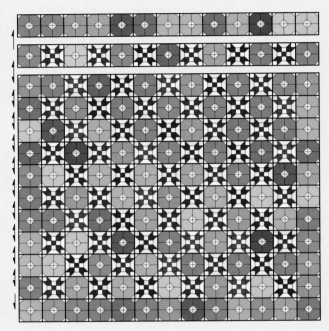

Quilt assembly

FINISHING THE QUILT

Refer to "Preparing to Quilt" on page 117, "Quilting Techniques" on page 118, and "Finishing Techniques" on page 119 for more detailed instructions, if needed.

1. Piece the quilt backing so that it is 4" to 6" longer and wider than the quilt top. Mark the quilt top if necessary. Layer the quilt top with batting and backing and baste the layers together—unless you plan to take your quilt to a long-arm quilter.

2. Hand or machine quilt as desired.

3. Trim the batting and backing even with the edges of the quilt top. Add a hanging sleeve if desired. Using the assorted red 2½"-wide strips, prepare the binding and sew it to the quilt. Make a label and attach it to the back of the quilt.

POPPY PATCH

By Anne Moscicki for Touchwood Quilt Design. Quilted by
Celeste Marshall of Cedar Grove Quilting.

In The Wizard of Oz, Dorothy fell asleep while crossing a field of poppies, but that won't happen to you while you're making these lively flowers—you'll be having too much fun!

MATERIALS

Finished quilt size: 48" x 61½"
Finished block size: 13½" x 13½"

Yardage is based on 42"-wide fabric.

12 coordinating fat quarters in pink and orange tones for poppy petals and petal accents
1½ yards of medium green for background, border, and binding
1¼ yards of light green for leaves
⅜ yard of light peach for poppy centers
⅜ yard of medium pink for poppy center accent
3⅓ yards of fabric for backing
54" x 68" piece of batting

CUTTING

All measurements include ¼"-wide seam allowances. Cut all strips across the width of the fabric.

From the medium pink, cut:
• 4 strips, 2¾" x 42"; crosscut into 48 squares, 2¾" x 2¾"

From the light green, cut:
• 7 strips, 5⅜" x 42"; crosscut into 48 squares, 5⅜" x 5⅜"

From the light peach, cut:
• 2 strips, 5" x 42"; crosscut into 12 squares, 5" x 5"

From *each* of the 12 fat quarters, cut:
• 4 squares, 5⅜" x 5⅜" (48 *total*)
• 4 squares, 2¾" x 2¾" (48 *total*)

From the medium green, cut:
• 4 strips, 2¾" x 42"; crosscut into 48 squares, 2¾" x 2¾"
• 5 strips, 4" x 42"
• 6 strips, 2½" x 42"

MAKING THE BLOCKS

1. Draw a diagonal line on the wrong side of each medium pink 2¾" square and each light green 5⅜" square.

2. Align a marked medium pink square right sides together on opposite corners of each 5" light peach square as shown. Stitch on the marked lines. Trim ¼" from the stitched lines as shown. Press the resulting triangles out and press the seam allowances toward the triangles. Repeat on the opposite corners of each square. Make 12.

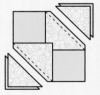
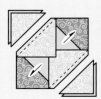

Make 12.

3. Referring to "Triangle Squares" on page 109, layer a marked light green 5⅜" square with each fat-quarter 5⅜" square. Mark, stitch, and cut to make eight triangle squares of each fat-quarter color (96 *total*). Press the seam allowances open.

Make 12 sets
of 8.

4. Using the eight matching triangle squares from one set, place matching fat-quarter 2¾" squares on the green half of four of the triangle squares, and dark green 2¾" squares on the remaining four triangle squares as shown, right sides together. Refer to step 2 to stitch on the marked lines, cut ¼" from the stitching line, and press the resulting triangles out. Press the seam allowances toward the small triangles. Repeat with the remaining sets of triangle squares.

Make 12 sets of 4 each.

5. Lay out the eight step 4 units from one set with a unit from step 2 in three rows as shown. Sew the units together in each row. Press the seam allowances open. Join the rows to complete the block. Press the seam allowances open. Repeat with the remaining sets to make 12 blocks *total*.

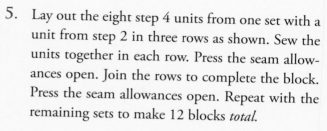

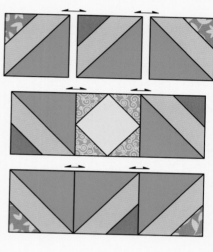

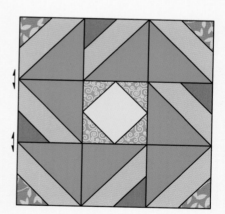

ASSEMBLING THE QUILT TOP

1. Arrange the blocks in four rows of three blocks each to create a pleasing layout. Join the blocks in each row. Press the seam allowances in opposite directions from row to row. Sew the rows together. Press the seam allowances in one direction.

2. Referring to "Borders with Butted Corners" on page 115, sew the medium green 4"-wide strips to the quilt top for the border.

FINISHING THE QUILT

Refer to "Preparing to Quilt" on page 117, "Quilting Techniques" on page 118, and "Finishing Techniques" on page 119 for more detailed instructions, if needed.

1. Piece the quilt backing so that it is 4" to 6" longer and wider than the quilt top. Mark the quilt top if necessary. Layer the quilt top with batting and backing, and baste the layers together—unless you plan to take your quilt to a long-arm quilter.

2. Hand or machine quilt as desired.

3. Trim the batting and backing even with the edges of the quilt top. Add a hanging sleeve if desired. Using the medium green 2½"-wide strips, prepare the binding and sew it to the quilt. Make a label and attach it to the back of the quilt.

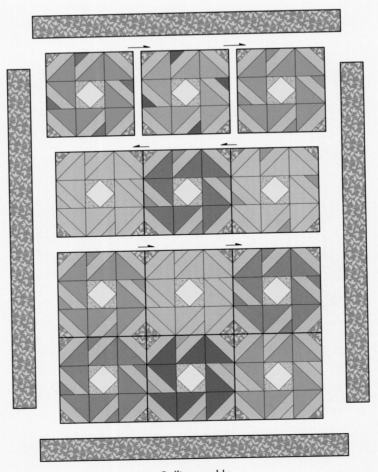

Quilt assembly

BLUEBERRY BUCKLE

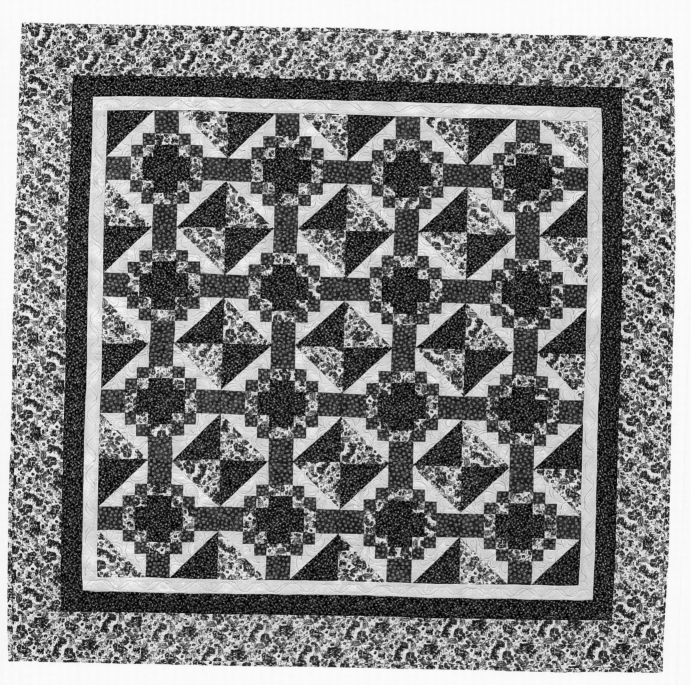

From Variations on a Theme *by Terry Martin.*
Pieced by Terry Martin and machine quilted by
Barb Dau.

With a block called Blueberry Buckle, what quilter can resist the urge to find just the right blueberry print to make it work? This cheerful quilt is worked in blue and yellow—a favorite color combination for quilters that has passed the test of time.

Finished quilt size: 54" x 54"
Finished block size: 10" x 10"

MATERIALS

Yardage is based on 42"-wide fabric.

2 yards of blueberry-and-yellow print for blocks, outer border, and binding
1 yard of dark blueberry print for blocks and middle border
⅞ yard of yellow print for blocks and inner border
¾ yard of green polka-dot print for blocks
3 yards of fabric for backing
60" x 60" piece of batting

CUTTING

All measurements include ¼"-wide seam allowances. Cut all strips across the width of the fabric.

From the green polka-dot print, cut:
- 4 strips, 2½" x 42"
- 6 strips, 1½" x 42"

From the blueberry-and-yellow print, cut:
- 5 strips, 1½" x 42"
- 2 strips, 4⅞" x 42"; crosscut into 16 squares, 4⅞" x 4⅞". Cut each square once diagonally to yield 2 half-square triangles (32 *total*).
- 6 strips, 4½" x 42"
- 6 strips, 2½" x 42"

From the dark blueberry print, cut:
- 1 strip, 4½" x 42"
- 2 strips, 1½" x 42"
- 2 strips, 4⅞" x 42"; crosscut into 16 squares, 4⅞" x 4⅞". Cut each square once diagonally to yield 2 half-square triangles (32 *total*).
- 5 strips, 2¼" x 42"

From the yellow print, cut:
- 5 strips, 1½" x 42"
- 5 strips, 2⅞" x 42"; crosscut into 64 squares, 2⅞" x 2⅞". Cut each square once diagonally to yield 2 half-square triangles (128 *total*).
- 5 strips, 1¾" x 42"

MAKING THE BLOCKS

1. Sew two green 2½" x 42" strips, two blueberry-and-yellow 1½" x 42" strips, and the dark blueberry 4½" x 42" strip together as shown to make a strip set. Press the seam allowances as indicated. Crosscut the strip set into 16 segments, 2½" wide.

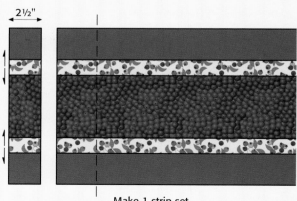

Make 1 strip set.
Cut 16 segments.

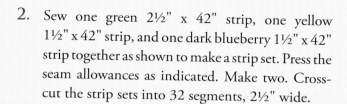

2. Sew one green 2½" x 42" strip, one yellow 1½" x 42" strip, and one dark blueberry 1½" x 42" strip together as shown to make a strip set. Press the seam allowances as indicated. Make two. Crosscut the strip sets into 32 segments, 2½" wide.

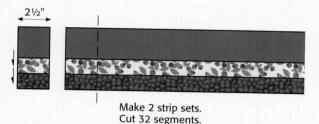

2½"

Make 2 strip sets.
Cut 32 segments.

3. Sew one green 1½" x 42" strip and one yellow 1½" x 42" strip together to make a strip set. Press the seam allowance toward the green strip. Make three. Repeat using a green 1½" x 42" strip and a blueberry-and-yellow 1½" x 42" strip. Make three strip sets. Crosscut 64 segments, 1½" wide, from each set of strip sets (128 *total*).

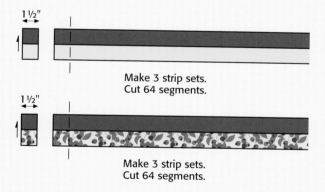

1½"

1½"

Make 3 strip sets.
Cut 64 segments.

Make 3 strip sets.
Cut 64 segments.

4. Sew one segment of each color combination from step 3 together as shown to make a four-patch unit. Press the seam allowances in one direction. Make 64.

Make 64.

5. Sew a yellow half-square triangle to two adjacent sides of each four-patch unit from step 4 as shown. Press the seam allowances toward the triangles. Make 64.

Make 64.

6. Sew a dark blueberry half-square triangle to the long edge of a unit from step 5 as shown. Make 32. Sew a blueberry-and-yellow half-square triangle to each remaining unit from step 5. Make 32. Press the seam allowances toward the half-square triangles.

Make 32 of each.

7. Sew one of each unit from step 6 to opposite sides of each segment from step 2 as shown. Press the seam allowances toward the step 6 units. Make 32.

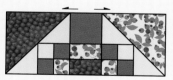

Make 32.

8. Sew each segment from step 1 between two units from step 7 as shown. Press the seam allowances toward the step 1 units. Make 16.

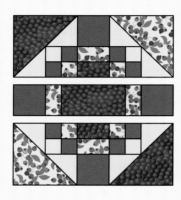

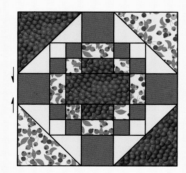

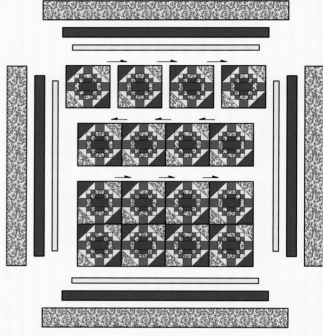

Make 16.

ASSEMBLING THE QUILT TOP

1. Refer to the quilt assembly diagram to arrange the blocks in four rows of four blocks each. Sew the blocks into rows. Press the seam allowances in opposite directions from row to row. Sew the rows together. Press the seam allowances in one direction.

2. Referring to "Borders with Butted Corners" on page 115, sew the yellow 1¾"-wide strips to the quilt top for the inner border. Measure the quilt for the middle border. Sew the dark blueberry 2¼"-wide strips to the quilt top in the same manner as the inner border. Repeat to add the blueberry-and-yellow 4½"-wide strips to the quilt top for the outer border.

Quilt assembly

FINISHING THE QUILT

Refer to "Preparing to Quilt" on page 117, "Quilting Techniques" on page 118, and "Finishing Techniques" on page 119 for more detailed instructions, if needed.

1. Piece the quilt backing so that it is 4" to 6" longer and wider than the quilt top. Mark the quilt top if necessary. Layer the quilt top with batting and backing, and baste the layers together—unless you plan to take your quilt to a long-arm quilter.

2. Hand or machine quilt as desired.

3. Trim the batting and backing even with the edges of the quilt top. Add a hanging sleeve if desired. Using the blueberry-and-yellow 2½"-wide strips, prepare the binding and sew it to the quilt. Make a label and attach it to the back of the quilt.

YOU SAY GOODBYE, I SAY HELLO

From Scraps of Time *by Ann Frischkorn and Amy Sandrin. Pieced and quilted by Amy Sandrin.*

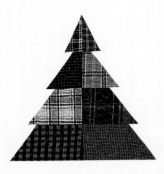

In a move from Colorado to Washington State, the maker of this quilt traded in the Rocky Mountains for the Pacific Northwest. While the two states have their differences, they share a lot of qualities, such as abundant forests and wildlife. The designer tried to capture the essence of both in this quilt by using recycled flannel shirts.

Finished quilt size: 60" x 64"
Finished block size: 16" x 16"

MATERIALS

Yardage is based on 38"-wide fabric.

1⅝ yards of light blue flannel for Tree blocks

1⅝ yards *total* of assorted green plaid flannels for Tree blocks

1¼ yards *total* of assorted plaid flannels for Bear's Paw blocks

1¼ yards of beige flannel for Bear's Paw blocks

¼ yard *each* of 5 different solid flannels for Bear's Paw block borders

¼ yard of dark green flannel for Bear's Paw blocks

1⅛ yards of dark blue flannel for outer border

⅝ yard of medium brown flannel for middle border

¾ yard of green plaid homespun fabric for binding

3⅝ yards of flannel for backing

66" x 70" piece of batting

Template plastic

Sharp pencil or marking tool

CUTTING

All measurements include ½"-wide seam allowances. Cut all strips across the width of the fabric. Trace the template patterns A–H on pages 78–81 onto template plastic and cut them out. Use the templates to cut out the pieces as indicated.

From the light blue flannel, cut:
- 6 strips, 5" x 38". From the strips, cut:
    4 template A pieces
    4 template A reversed pieces
    4 template C pieces
    4 template C reversed pieces
    4 template E pieces
    4 template E reversed pieces
- 2 strips, 4½" x 38". From the strips, cut:
    4 template G pieces
    4 template G reversed pieces
- 3 strips, 3¾" x 38"; crosscut the strips into 24 squares, 3¾" x 3¾"

From the assorted green plaid flannels, cut a *total* of:
- 4 template B pieces
- 4 template B reversed pieces
- 4 template D pieces
- 4 template D reversed pieces
- 4 template F pieces
- 4 template F reversed pieces
- 4 template H pieces
- 4 template H reversed pieces
- 24 squares, 3¾" x 3¾"

From the beige flannel, cut:
- 80 squares, 3" x 3"
- 40 squares, 3¾" x 3¾"

From the assorted plaid flannels, cut a *total* of:
- 20 sets, consisting of 2 squares, 3¾" x 3¾", and 4 squares, 3" x 3". Each set should be cut from the same plaid fabric.

From the dark green flannel, cut:
- 5 squares, 3" x 3"

From _each_ of the 5 different solid flannels, cut:
- 2 strips, 2" x 15" (10 _total_)
- 2 strips, 2" x 17" (10 _total_)

From the medium brown flannel, cut:
- 6 strips, 3" x 38"

From the dark blue flannel, cut:
- 7 strips, 5" x 38"

From the green plaid homespun fabric, cut:
- 7 strips, 2¾" x 38"

MAKING THE TREE BLOCKS

Use a ½" seam allowance when sewing pieces together.

1. Sew the light blue template pieces to the assorted green plaid template pieces as shown to make the Tree-block units. Make four of each unit.

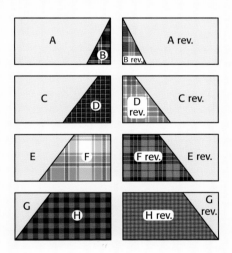

2. Arrange one of each unit into four rows as shown. Sew the units in each row together. Press the seam allowances in alternate directions from row to row. Sew the rows together. Make four Tree blocks.

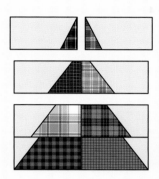 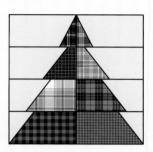

Tree block.
Make 4.

MAKING THE BEAR'S PAW BLOCKS

1. Draw a line from corner to corner on the wrong side of each beige 3¾" square. Place each marked square right sides together with an assorted plaid 3¾" square (do not use the green plaid squares at this time). Sew ½" from both sides of the marked lines. Cut the squares apart on the marked lines. Each layered square will yield two triangle-square units. Press the seam allowances toward the plaid fabric. Make 20 sets of four matching triangle-square units (80 _total_).

Make 20 sets
of 4 each.

2. Arrange 16 beige 3" squares, one dark green 3" square, four groups of four matching triangle-square units, and four groups of four matching plaid 3" squares that match the triangle-square units into seven rows as shown. Sew the squares in each row together. Press the seam allowances in opposite directions from row to row. Sew the rows together. Press the seam allowances in one direction. Make five.

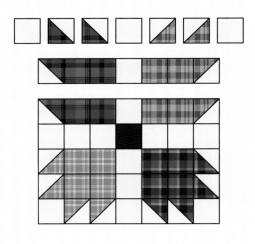

Make 5.

3. Sew matching solid flannel 2" x 15" strips to the top and bottom of each step 2 unit. Press the seam allowances toward the strips. Sew the matching solid flannel 2" x 17" strips to the sides of each unit. Press the seam allowances toward the strips to complete the five Bear's Paw blocks.

 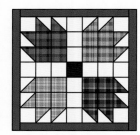

Bear's Paw block.
Make 5.

ASSEMBLING THE QUILT TOP

1. Refer to the quilt assembly diagram on page 77 to lay out the blocks in three rows of three blocks each, alternating the Bear's Paw blocks with the Tree blocks.

2. Sew the blocks in each row together. Press the seam allowances in opposite directions from row to row. Sew the rows together. Press the seam allowances in one direction.

3. Use a sharp pencil or marking tool to draw a line from corner to corner on the wrong side of each light blue 3¾" square. Place each marked square right sides together with an assorted green plaid 3¾" square. Sew ½" from both sides of the marked lines. Cut the squares apart on the marked lines. Each layered square will yield two triangle-square units. Press the seam allowances toward the plaid fabric. Make 48.

4. Sew 24 triangle-square units together into one row as shown. Press the seam allowances in one direction. Make two rows.

Make 2.

5. Sew the rows to the top and bottom edges of the quilt top so that the points are facing up. Press the seam allowances toward the blocks.

6. Sew the brown 3" x 38" strips together end to end into one long strip. From the pieced strip, cut two strips, 3" x 49", and sew them to the top and bottom of the quilt. Press the seam allowances toward the borders. From the remainder of the pieced strip, cut two strips, 3" x 53", and sew them to the sides of the quilt. Press the seam allowances toward the borders.

Note that because flannel stretches so much, it's better to use the measurement of what the blocks should be, following the cutting instructions, instead of the center measurements of the actual quilt, to determine the border-strip lengths.

7. Sew the dark blue 5" x 38" strips together end to end into one long strip. From the pieced strip, cut two strips, 5" x 53", and sew them to the top and bottom of the quilt. Press the seam allowances toward the outer borders. From the remainder of the pieced strip, cut two strips, 5" x 65", and sew them to the sides of the quilt. Press the seam allowances toward the outer borders.

FINISHING THE QUILT

Refer to "Preparing to Quilt" on page 117, "Quilting Techniques" on page 118, and "Finishing Techniques" on page 119 for more detailed instructions, if needed.

1. Piece the quilt backing so that it is 4" to 6" longer and wider than the quilt top. Mark the quilt top if necessary. Layer the quilt top with batting and backing, and baste the layers together—unless you plan to take your quilt to a long-arm quilter.

2. Hand or machine quilt as desired.

3. Trim the batting and backing even with the edges of the quilt top. Add a hanging sleeve if desired. Using the green plaid homespun 2¾"-wide strips, prepare the binding and sew it to the quilt. Make a label and attach it to the back of the quilt.

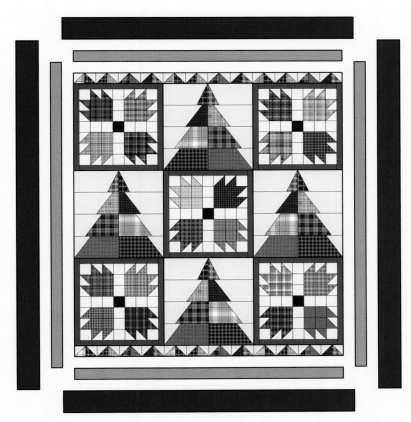

Quilt assembly

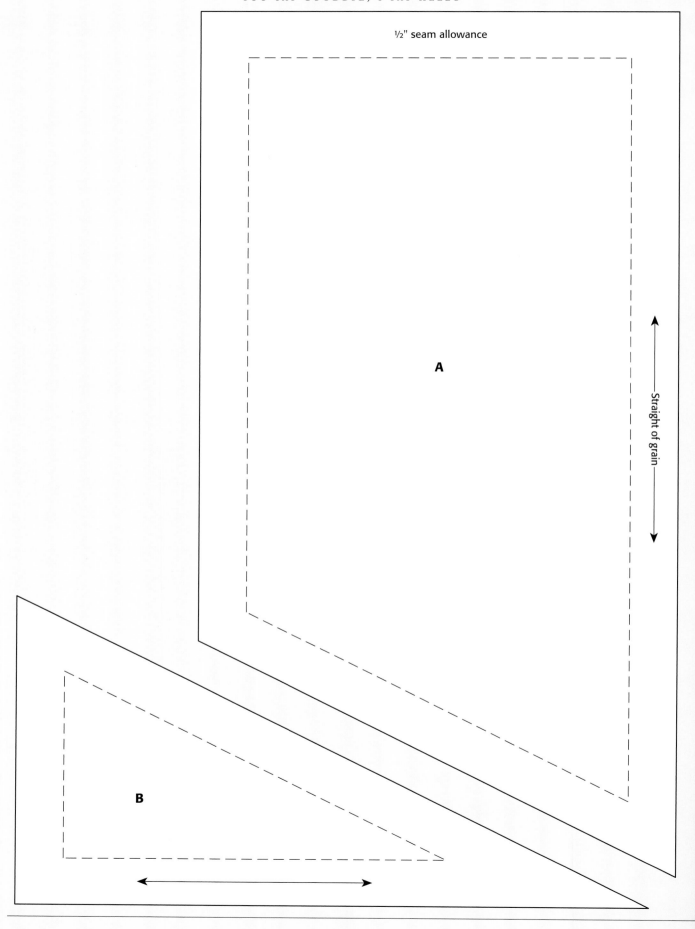

½" seam allowance

A

Straight of grain

B

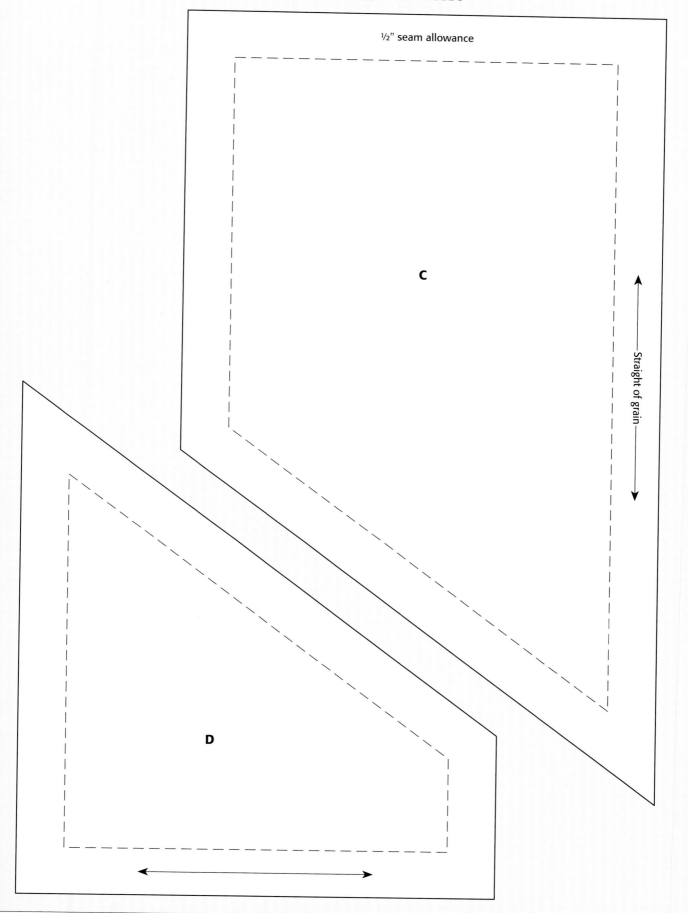

½" seam allowance

C

Straight of grain

D

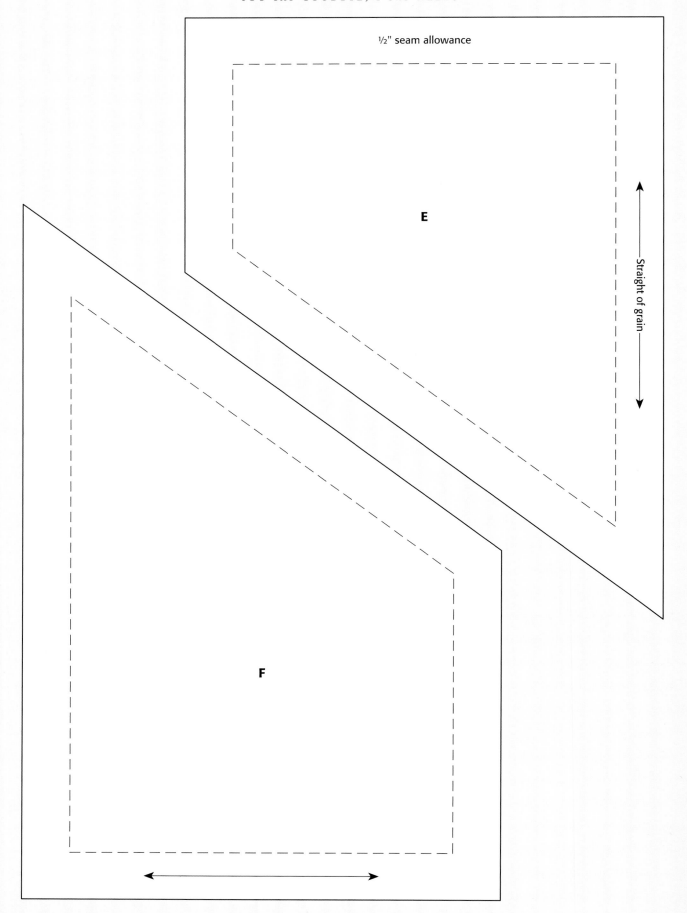

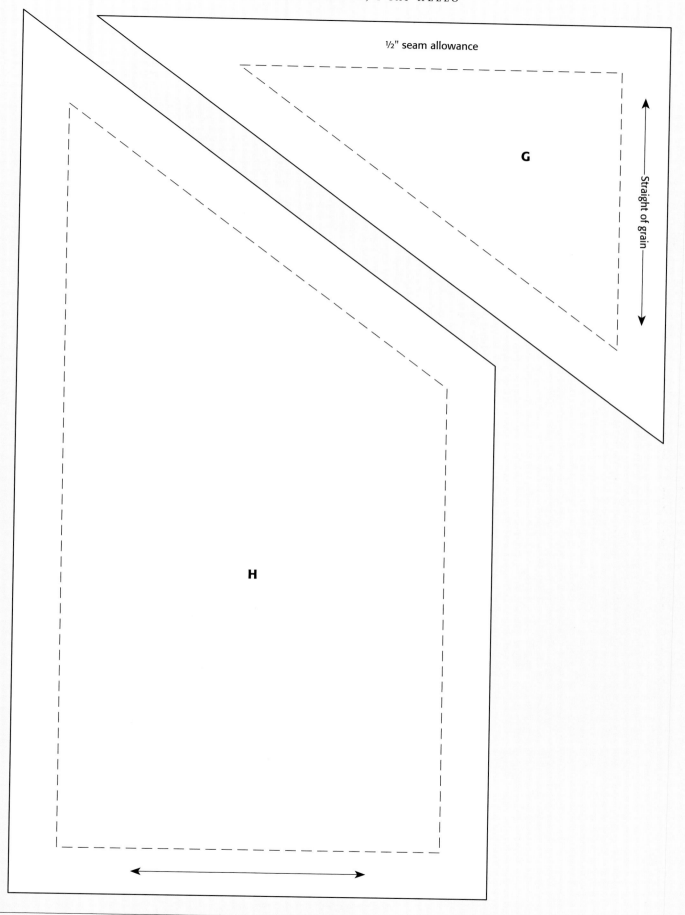

½" seam allowance

G

Straight of grain

H

WATERFALLS

From Big 'n Easy *by Judy Hopkins. Pieced by*
Martha M. Morris and quilted by Tracey Dukowitz.

Diagonal lines of light fabric cascade gently through an assortment of dark prints to create this lovely quilt. Though they look complicated, the blocks are easily made by cutting segments from just two different strip sets and then turning them so the light portions form the pattern.

Finished quilt size: 98" x 98"
Finished block size: 9" x 9"

MATERIALS

Yardage is based on 42"-wide fabric.

⅜ yard *each* of 16 assorted dark prints (blues, greens, and purples) for blocks

4¾ yards of multicolored print for inner border, outer border, and binding*

3⅛ yards of cream print for blocks and middle border

9⅝ yards of fabric for backing

104" x 104" piece of batting

Use the same fabric as one of the assorted dark prints, if you wish.

CUTTING

All measurements include ¼"-wide seam allowances. Cut all strips across the width of the fabric unless otherwise indicated.

From *each* of the 16 assorted dark prints, cut:
- 2 strips, 5" x 42" (32 *total*)
- 1 strip, 2" x 42" (16 *total*)

From the cream print, cut:
- 50 strips, 2" x 42". Set 10 of the strips aside for the middle border. Cut 8 of the strips in half widthwise to make 16 strips, 2" x 21".

From the multicolored print, cut:
- 10 strips, 3½" x 42"
- 11 strips, 2½" x 42"

From the *lengthwise grain* of the remaining multicolored print, cut:
4 strips, 9" wide x at least 92" long

MAKING THE BLOCKS

This is one of those designs that creates an occasional pressing conundrum no matter what you do. If you press the seam allowances open, you may have difficulty matching seams, and you'll have no "ditch" to stitch in when you reach the quilting stage. If you press to the side, you may have to twist some seams on the back when you assemble the blocks and/or the quilt, to make them butt together properly for easy joining. You choose.

1. Cut *one* 5" x 42" strip of *each* of the assorted dark prints in half crosswise to make two strips, 5" x 21". Trim one 5" x 21" strip to 3½" wide, as shown. You'll have a total of 16 strips, 5" x 21", and 16 strips, 3½" x 21".

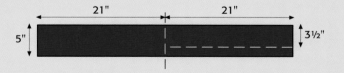

2. Join two cream 2" x 42" strips, a dark print 2" x 42" strip, and a matching dark print 5" x 42" strip to make one strip set as shown. Press the seam allowances open or toward the dark prints. From this strip set, cut 16 segments, 2" wide.

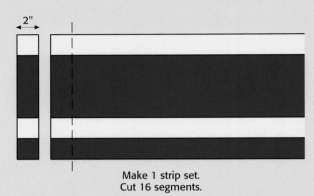

Make 1 strip set.
Cut 16 segments.

3. Using the same dark print as in step 1, join a dark 3½" x 21" strip, a cream 2" x 21" strip, and a dark 5" x 21" strip to make one strip set, as shown. Press the seam allowances open or toward the dark prints. From this strip set, cut eight segments, 2" wide.

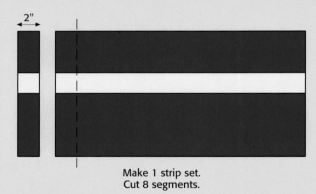

Make 1 strip set.
Cut 8 segments.

4. Join the step 2 and step 3 segments to make four blocks as shown. Press the seam allowances open or all in one direction.

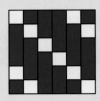

Make 4.

5. Repeat steps 2–4 with the remaining dark 2"-, 3½"-, and 5"-wide strips and the cream 2"-wide strips to make 64 blocks total. Once you know what you're doing, you can work with several combinations of cream and dark fabrics at once. *Just remember that each finished block should contain only two fabrics—the cream print and one of the assorted dark prints.*

ASSEMBLING THE QUILT TOP

1. Join the blocks to make 16 four-block units exactly as shown. Combine the fabrics at random. Press the seam allowances open or to one side.

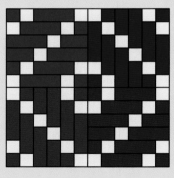

Make 16.

2. Join the blocks to make four rows of four blocks each. Press the seam allowances in opposite directions from row to row.

3. Join the rows. Press the seam allowances however you wish.

4. Referring to "Borders with Butted Corners" on page 115, measure the quilt top for the inner border. Trim the 9"-wide multicolored strips to the length measured and sew them to the quilt top. Measure the quilt for the middle border. Sew the cream 2"-wide strips to the quilt in the same manner as the inner border. Repeat to add the multicolored 3½"-wide strips to the quilt top for the outer border.

FINISHING THE QUILT

Refer to "Preparing to Quilt" on page 117, "Quilting Techniques" on page 118, and "Finishing Techniques" on page 119 for more detailed instructions, if needed.

1. Piece the quilt backing so that it is 4" to 6" longer and wider than the quilt top. Mark the quilt top if necessary. Layer the quilt top with batting and backing, and baste the layers together—unless you plan to take your quilt to a long-arm quilter.

2. Hand or machine quilt as desired.

3. Trim the batting and backing even with the edges of the quilt top. Add a hanging sleeve if desired. Using the multicolored print 2½"-wide strips, prepare the binding and sew it to the quilt. Make a label and attach it to the back of the quilt.

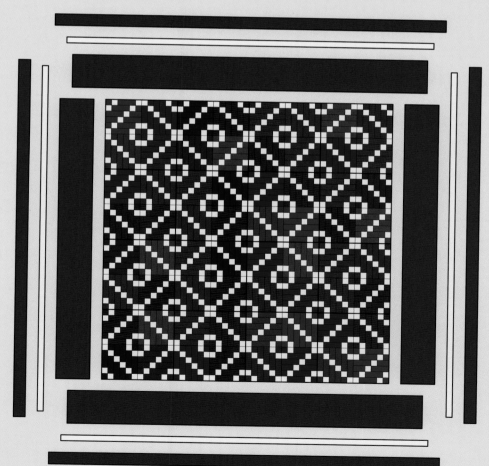

Quilt assembly

SUMMER'S END

From New Cuts for New Quilts *by*
Karla Alexander

This quilt is made by stacking several fabrics into a deck and then randomly cutting through the deck at various angles. The pieces in each deck are then shuffled to create an assortment of different-looking blocks.

Finished quilt size: 49½" x 67½"
Finished block size: 6" x 6"

MATERIALS

Yardage is based on 42"-wide fabric.

⅓ yard *each* of 8 assorted red and 8 assorted blue fabrics
    for blocks (16 fabrics *total*)
1⅛ yards of blue batik for outer border
½ yard of light blue fabric for inner border
Assorted red, gold, and brown scraps for leaves
⅝ yard of fabric for binding
3⅛ yards of fabric for backing
55" x 73" piece of batting
¾ yard of paper-backed fusible web

CUTTING

All measurements include ¼"-wide seam allowances. Cut all strips across the width of the fabric.

From *each* red and blue fabric for blocks, cut:
* 1 strip, 7¼" x 42"; crosscut into 4 rectangles,
  7¼" x 10" (64 *total*; 8 left over)

From the light blue inner-border fabric, cut:
* 6 strips, 2" x 42"

From the blue batik, cut:
* 6 strips, 5½" x 42"

From the binding fabric, cut:
* 7 strips, 2½" x 42"

ARRANGING, CUTTING, AND SHUFFLING THE DECKS

1. Arrange the 7¼" x 10" assorted red rectangles into four decks of seven rectangles each, right sides up. Each deck should contain a different mix of fabrics. Secure each deck with a pin through all the layers. Repeat with the assorted blue fabrics.

2. Working with one deck at a time, cut the deck into seven pieces as shown in the block diagram. Vary the width and angle of the cuts from deck to deck so that all decks are cut a little differently from one another. As you go, secure each deck to a piece of paper by pinning through all the layers.

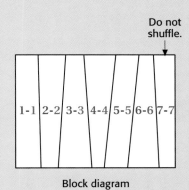

Block diagram

3. Now we're going to shuffle the decks. The segment stack number is shown on the illustration above in red. Working with one deck, remove the top layer from the segment 1 stack and place it on the bottom of the stack. Remove two layers from the segment 2 stack and place them on the bottom of the stack. Remove three layers from the segment 3 stack and place them on the bottom of the stack. Continue shuffling each stack

in this way, removing the same number of fabrics from the top as the number of the segment you are shuffling. You do not need to shuffle the last segment stack.

4. Once you've completed the shuffling process, re-assemble the deck and pin each stack of segments to a piece of paper through all the layers. Be sure to keep the segment stacks in the exact order and layout in which you shuffled them. Once the segments are secure, use a pencil and trace along the cutting lines onto the paper. The pins will help keep the segments in order, and the lines will create a template reference.

5. Repeat steps 3 and 4 to shuffle the remaining decks.

THE BLUE NUMBERS shown on the block diagram on page 87 indicate the sewing order. It is important that you keep the segment stacks in their shuffled order while sewing; otherwise you'll end up duplicating a fabric within the same block. For instance, after chain piecing all layers of the segment 1 stack and the segment 2 stack together, always return the units to their original order. It's easy to reverse the order while ironing and/or clipping the segments apart, so *I strongly recommend that you place a safety pin in the top layer of the segment 1 stack.* That way, when you begin sewing again, you'll automatically know the combined segments are in the right sequence if the safety pin is on the top of the stack. If the safety pin is not on top of the stack, you'll know you probably reversed the order and you will need to correct it before you continue. Keep the safety pin in place until you've sewn all the blocks in the deck.

MAKING THE BLOCKS

1. Unpin the segment 1 and 2 stacks from one deck and peel off the top pieces from each stack. Flip piece 2 onto piece 1 with right sides facing, and stitch the pieces together. Without removing the previous pair, pick up the next layer from the segment 1 and 2 stacks and sew them together in the same manner. Continue chain piecing the pairs together until you've stitched all the segment 1 and segment 2 pieces together.

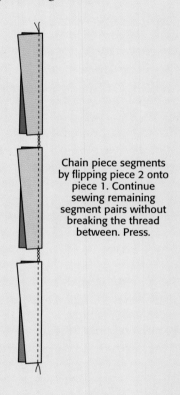

Chain piece segments by flipping piece 2 onto piece 1. Continue sewing remaining segment pairs without breaking the thread between. Press.

2. Press the 1-2 units open with the seam allowance to either side. Then clip the units apart and restack them in their original order.

3. Unpin the segment 3 stack. Peel off the top piece from stack 3 and sew it, right sides together, to the top 1-2 unit. Again, you can chain piece the units. Don't be surprised if the new edges of additional segments don't line up evenly with the combined units; they more than likely will not. Just match them together as best as you can, making sure your seam is at least ¼" from the raw edges.

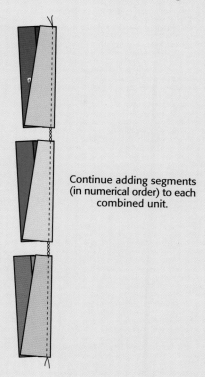

Continue adding segments (in numerical order) to each combined unit.

4. Press the units open with the seam allowance to either side, clip them apart, and stack them in their original order. Continue adding segments in numerical order until you've added all the segments.

5. Repeat the process with the remaining decks to make 28 red blocks and 28 blue blocks. Trim the blocks to 6½" x 6½". *It's OK if your block dimensions are a little larger or smaller; just be sure to trim all the blocks to the same size.*

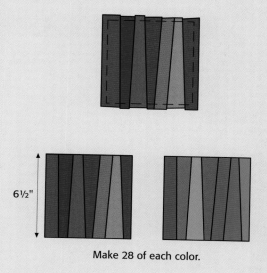

6½"

Make 28 of each color.

ASSEMBLING THE QUILT TOP

1. Refer to the quilt assembly diagram on page 90 to arrange the blocks into six vertical rows of nine blocks each, alternating the red and the blue blocks as shown. (You will have one block of each color left over. Set these aside for another project.) Place the red blocks so that the seams run horizontally and the blue blocks so that the seams run vertically. If possible, view your arrangement through a door peephole to check the color and block balance. Sew the blocks in each row together. Press the seam allowances in opposite directions from row to row. Sew the rows together. Press the seam allowances in one direction.

2. Referring to "Borders with Butted Corners" on page 115, sew the light blue strips to the quilt top for the inner border. Measure the quilt top for the outer border. Sew the blue batik strips to the quilt top in the same manner as the inner borders.

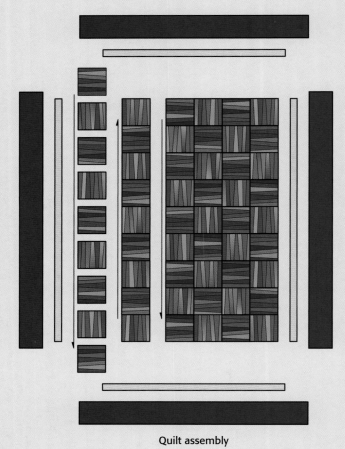

Quilt assembly

ADDING THE APPLIQUÉS

1. Referring to "Fusible Appliqué" on page 113, trace a total of 11 leaf patterns on page 91 onto the paper side of the fusible web. Cut around the shapes and fuse them to the wrong sides of the assorted red, gold, and brown scraps. Cut out the appliqué shapes on the marked lines.

2. Remove the paper backing from the appliqué shapes. Referring to the quilt photo on page 86, position and fuse the appliqués to the borders. Hand or machine stitch around each appliqué using your preferred stitch.

FINISHING THE QUILT

Refer to "Preparing to Quilt" on page 117, "Quilting Techniques" on page 118, and "Finishing Techniques" on page 119 for more detailed instructions, if needed.

1. Piece the quilt backing so that it is 4" to 6" longer and wider than the quilt top. Mark the quilt top if necessary. Layer the quilt top with batting and backing, and baste the layers together—unless you plan to take your quilt to a long-arm quilter.

2. Hand or machine quilt as desired.

3. Trim the batting and backing even with the edges of the quilt top. Add a hanging sleeve if desired. Using the 2½"-wide binding strips, prepare the binding and sew it to the quilt. Make a label and attach it to the back of the quilt.

Appliqué patterns

Patterns do not include seam allowances.
Patterns are reversed for fusible appliqué.

A BOUQUET OF STARS

From Clever Quarters, Too *by Susan Teegarden Dissmore. Designed and pieced by Susan Teegarden Dissmore. Machine quilted by Eileen Peacher.*

If your collection of fat quarters could use some thinning, here is the perfect pattern—this stellar design uses 30 fat quarters! To maintain continuity between the blocks, one beige print was used for the background of the blocks and the inner and middle borders, and a floral print was selected for the center of each block and the outer border.

Finished quilt size: 80" x 100"
Finished block size: 10" x 10"

MATERIALS

Yardage is based on 42"-wide fabric.

3 yards of beige print for blocks, inner border, and middle border

4 fat quarters *each* of assorted dark red, dark green, and dark blue prints for blocks (12 fat quarters *total*)

8 fat quarters of assorted black prints for blocks, inner border, and middle border*

7 fat quarters of assorted medium tan prints for blocks, inner border, and middle border

1¾ yards of floral print for block centers and outer border

1¼ yards of navy tone-on-tone print for outer border

3 fat quarters of assorted light tan tone-on-tone prints for blocks

⅞ yard of fabric for binding

7½ yards of fabric for backing

88" x 108" piece of batting

More than one fat quarter of the same print was included in the assortment.

CUTTING

All measurements include ¼"-wide seam allowances. Cut all strips across the width of the fabric.

From the beige print, cut:

- 7 strips, 6¼" x 42"; crosscut into 41 squares, 6¼" x 6¼". Cut each square twice diagonally to yield 164 triangles (2 left over).
- 4 strips, 3⅜" x 42"; crosscut into 38 squares, 3⅜" x 3⅜". Cut each square once diagonally to yield 76 triangles.
- 14 strips, 3" x 42"; crosscut into:
    52 squares, 3" x 3"
    14 rectangles, 3" x 15½"
    28 rectangles, 3" x 5½"

From *each* of the 3 light tan tone-on-tone prints, cut:

- 2 strips, 6¼" x 21"; crosscut into 4 squares, 6¼" x 6¼". Cut each square twice diagonally to yield 16 triangles (48 *total*).
- 1 strip, 3⅜" x 21"; crosscut into 5 squares, 3⅜" x 3⅜". Cut each square once diagonally to yield 10 triangles (30 *total*).
- 3 squares, 3⅜" x 3⅜"; cut each square once diagonally to yield 6 triangles (18 *total*)

From *each* of the 12 dark red, dark green, and dark blue prints, cut:

- 3 strips, 3⅜" x 21"; crosscut into 12 squares, 3⅜" x 3⅜". Cut each square once diagonally to yield 24 triangles (288 *total*).
- 1 square, 6¼" x 6¼"; cut the square twice diagonally to yield 4 triangles (48 *total*)

Continued on page 94

Continued from page 93

From the floral print, cut:
- 3 strips, 11¼" x 42"; crosscut into 7 squares, 11¼" x 11¼". Cut each square twice diagonally to yield 28 triangles.
- 1 strip, 5⅞" x 42"; crosscut into 6 squares, 5⅞" x 5⅞". Cut each square once diagonally to yield 12 triangles.

From the remainder of the floral print, selectively cut:
- 12 squares, 5½" x 5½"

From *each* of 6 medium tan prints, cut:
- 4 strips, 3⅜" x 21"; crosscut into:
  16 squares, 3⅜" x 3⅜"; cut each square once diagonally to yield 32 triangles (192 *total*)
  5 squares, 3" x 3" (30 *total*)
- 1 strip, 3" x 21"; crosscut into 6 squares, 3" x 3" (36 *total*)

From the remaining medium tan print, cut:
- 3 strips, 3" x 21"; crosscut into 14 squares, 3" x 3"

From *each* of 4 black prints, cut:
- 5 strips, 3⅜" x 21"; crosscut into 24 squares, 3⅜" x 3⅜". Cut each square once diagonally to yield 48 triangles (192 *total*)

From *each* of the remaining 4 black prints, cut:
- 1 square, 6¼" x 6¼"; cut each square twice diagonally to yield 4 triangles (16 *total*; 2 left over)
- 7 squares, 3" x 3" (28 *total*)
- 1 strip, 3⅜" x 21"; crosscut into 5 squares, 3⅜" x 3⅜". Cut each square once diagonally to yield 10 triangles (40 *total*; 4 left over).

From the navy tone-on-tone print, cut:
- 3 strips, 11¼" x 42"; crosscut into 8 squares, 11¼" x 11¼". Cut each square twice diagonally to yield 32 triangles.
- 1 strip, 5⅞" x 42"; crosscut into 2 squares, 5⅞" x 5⅞". Cut each square once diagonally to yield 4 triangles.

From the binding fabric, cut:
- 10 strips, 2½" x 42"

MAKING THE BLOCKS

1. Using the triangles cut from 3⅜" squares, sew a beige triangle to a light tan tone-on-tone triangle along their longest edges to form a triangle square. Make 12 sets of four matching triangle squares (48 *total*). Press the seam allowances toward the light tan triangles and trim the dog-ears.

Make 48
in matching
sets of 4.

2. Referring to "Flying-Geese Units" on page 110, sew two matching dark red triangles cut from 3⅜" squares to the short edges of a beige triangle cut from a 6¼" square. Make four sets of four matching flying-geese units (16 *total*). Repeat with the dark green and dark blue triangles cut from 3⅜" squares. Press the seam allowances toward the dark triangles and trim the dog-ears.

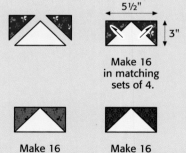

Make 16
in matching
sets of 4.

Make 16
in matching
sets of 4.

Make 16
in matching
sets of 4.

3. Arrange and sew the units from steps 1 and 2 and the floral print 5½" squares together into rows as shown. (The flying-geese units for each block should use the same dark fabric.) Press the seam allowances as indicated. Sew the rows together to make the Magic Cross blocks in the color

combinations shown. Press the seam allowances as indicated.

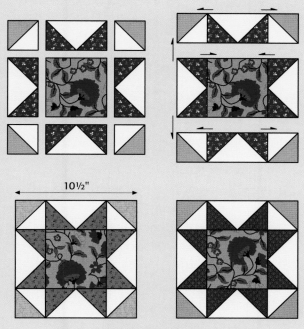

10½"

Magic Cross blocks.
Make 4 of each color combination.

4. Using the triangles cut from 3⅜" squares, refer to step 1 to make triangle squares from the medium tan, dark red, dark green, and dark blue triangles as shown. Press the seam allowances toward the dark triangles and trim the dog-ears. Make four sets of eight matching triangle squares (32 *total*) of each color combination.

 3"

Make 32 in matching sets of 8.   Make 32 in matching sets of 8.   Make 32 in matching sets of 8.

5. Sew the remaining dark red, dark green, and dark blue triangles cut from 3⅜" squares to the light tan tone-on-tone triangles cut from 6¼" squares to make flying-geese units. Make four sets of four matching flying-geese units (16 *total*) of each

color combination. Press the seam allowances toward the dark triangles and trim the dog-ears.

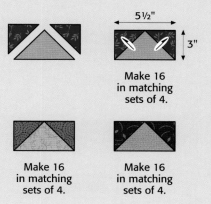

5½"   3"

Make 16 in matching sets of 4.

Make 16 in matching sets of 4.   Make 16 in matching sets of 4.

6. Sew the medium tan triangles cut from 3⅜" squares to the short edges of the dark red, dark green, and dark blue triangles cut from 6¼" squares to make flying-geese units. Make four sets of four flying-geese units (16 *total*) of each color combination. Press the seam allowances toward the medium tan triangles and trim the dog-ears.

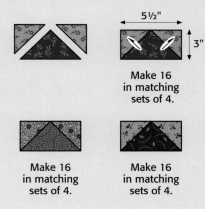

5½"   3"

Make 16 in matching sets of 4.

Make 16 in matching sets of 4.   Make 16 in matching sets of 4.

7. Sew the black triangles cut from 3⅜" squares to the short edges of the beige triangles cut from 6¼" squares. Press the seam allowances toward the black triangles and trim the dog-ears.

5½"   3"

Make 114.

8. Sew the units from steps 4–7 and the 3" squares cut from the beige and medium tan prints together as shown to form the frames. (The dark red, dark green, and dark blue fabrics in each frame should match.) Press the seam allowances as indicated. Sew the frames to a like-colored Magic Cross block from step 3 to complete the framed blocks. Press the seam allowances as indicated. Make four blocks of each color and press the final seam allowances open.

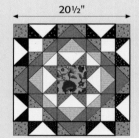 

20½"

Framed Magic Cross blocks.
Make 4 of each.

ASSEMBLING THE QUILT TOP

1. Referring to the quilt assembly diagram on page 98, arrange and sew the blocks into four rows of three blocks each as shown. Press the seam allowances open. Sew the rows together. Press the seam allowances open.

2. Sew the remaining beige triangles cut from 3⅜" squares to the short edges of 14 black triangles cut from 6¼" squares. Press the seam allowances toward the beige triangles and trim the dog-ears.

5½"

3"

Make 14.

3. With right sides together, place a black 3" square on the left-hand side of a beige 3" x 5½" rectangle. Draw a diagonal line through the square as shown and sew on the line. Leaving a ¼" seam allowance, trim away the excess fabric. Press the seam allowance toward the black print. Repeat to make 14 units.

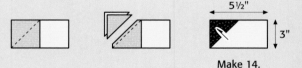

5½"

3"

Make 14.

4. Repeat step 3, sewing the remaining black squares to the right-hand side of the remaining beige 3" x 5½" rectangles.

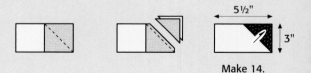

5½"

3"

Make 14.

5. Sew the units from steps 2–4 and the remaining medium tan 3" squares together as shown below to form the inner-border rows. Press the seam allowances as indicated.

Top/bottom inner border.
Make 2.

Side inner border.
Make 2.

6. Referring to the quilt assembly diagram on page 98, sew the side inner borders to the quilt top as shown. Press the seam allowances toward the borders. Sew the top and bottom inner borders to the quilt top. Press the seam allowances toward the borders.

7. Sew the remaining units from step 7 of "Making the Blocks" to the remaining beige 3" squares and the beige 3" x 15½" rectangles to form the middle borders. Press the seam allowances toward the beige squares and rectangles.

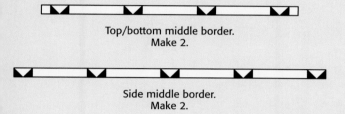

Top/bottom middle border.
Make 2.

Side middle border.
Make 2.

8. Referring to the quilt assembly diagram, sew the side middle borders to the quilt top as shown. Press the seam allowances toward the middle borders. Sew the top and bottom middle borders to the quilt top. Press the seam allowances toward the middle borders.

9. Using the triangles cut from 5⅞" squares, sew each navy triangle to a floral triangle along the longest edges to make triangle squares. Press the seam allowances toward the navy triangles and trim the dog-ears.

5½"

Make 4.

10. Sew the floral and navy triangles cut from 11¼" squares, the triangle squares from step 9, and the remaining floral triangles cut from the 5⅞" squares together as shown to form the outer-border rows. Press the seam allowances toward the navy triangles and the half-square-triangle units.

Top/bottom outer border.
Make 2.

Side outer border.
Make 2.

11. Referring to the quilt assembly diagram, sew the side outer borders to the quilt top as shown. Press the seam allowances toward the outer borders. Sew the top and bottom outer borders to the quilt top. Press the seam allowances toward the outer borders.

FINISHING THE QUILT

Refer to "Preparing to Quilt" on page 117, "Quilting Techniques" on page 118, and "Finishing Techniques" on page 119 for more detailed instructions, if needed.

1. Piece the quilt backing so that it is 4" to 6" longer and wider than the quilt top. Mark the quilt top if necessary. Layer the quilt top with batting and backing, and baste the layers together—unless you plan to take your quilt to a long-arm quilter.

2. Hand or machine quilt as desired.

3. Trim the batting and backing even with the edges of the quilt top. Add a hanging sleeve if desired. Using the 2½"-wide binding strips, prepare the binding and sew it to the quilt. Make a label and attach it to the back of the quilt.

Quilt assembly

HOW FAR IS IT TO BETHLEHEM?

From Adoration Quilts *by Rachel W. N. Brown.*
Pieced and appliquéd by Rachel W. N. Brown.
Machine quilted by Lyon Den Quilting.

This lap quilt brings together favorite images of that wondrous trip to Bethlehem: the star, the elegant travelers, and the camels. Gather the little ones in your family, cover them with this quilt, and read them the story of camels and traveling Wise Men.

Finished quilt size: 71½" x 55½"
Finished block size: 8" x 8"

MATERIALS

Yardage is based on 40"-wide fabric.

3¼ yards of multicolored batik stripe for outer border and binding*

½ yard of light brown mottled print for inner border

⅜ yard of gold print for Star blocks

¼ yard (or fat quarter) *each* of 8 assorted medium to dark blue prints for sky

⅛ yard (or fat eighth) *each* of 8 assorted light to medium brown prints for sand

Fat eighth of very light gold print for large Star block

9" x 9" square *each* of 3 different browns for *each* camel appliqué (9 squares *total*; 1–8)

6" x 9" piece *each* of 3 coordinating fabrics for *each* Wise Man appliqué (9 pieces *total*. First Wise Man: 4–11, 13, and 14. Second Wise Man: 2, 5, 6, 7, 9, and 10. Third Wise Man: 3, 4, 5, 8, 9, 12, and 13.)

3" x 9" piece of wood-grain print for staff appliqués (1, 2, and 15; 3; and 6)

3" x 6" piece of tan fabric for Wise Men's face (12; 8; and 10) and hand (3; 1 and 4; and 7) appliqués

3" x 3" squares of 12 to 15 different scraps for camel bundle appliqués (9–14)

Small scraps of black and gray prints for third Wise Man's shoes and beard (1, 2, and 11)

3¼ yards of fabric for backing

58" x 78" piece of batting

Black and gray embroidery floss

Three black seed beads

Assorted beads, small leather strips, tassels, and braided twine for embellishment (optional)

*A stripe that runs lengthwise works best.

CUTTING

All measurements include ¼"-wide seam allowances. Cut all strips across the width of the fabric unless otherwise indicated.

From the assorted medium to dark blue prints, cut a *total* of:
- 168 rectangles, 2½" x 4½"
- 28 squares, 1⅞" x 1⅞"
- 28 squares, 1½" x 1½"
- 4 squares, 2⅞" x 2⅞"
- 4 squares, 2½" x 2½"

From the assorted light to medium brown prints, cut a *total* of:
- 90 rectangles, 2½" x 4½"

From the gold print, cut:
- 4 squares, 2⅞" x 2⅞"
- 2 strips, 1⅞" x 40"; crosscut into 32 squares, 1⅞" x 1⅞"
- 1 strip, 2½" x 40"; crosscut into 8 squares, 2½" x 2½"

From the very light gold print, cut:
- 4 squares, 1⅞" x 1⅞"
- 4 squares, 1½" x 1½"

From the light brown mottled print, cut:
- 6 strips, 2" x 40"

From the *lengthwise grain* of the multicolored batik stripe, cut:
- 2 strips, 6½" x 60"
- 2 strips, 6½" x 76"

From the remaining multicolored batik stripe, cut:
- 2½"-wide bias strips to make a 265" length of binding

MAKING THE SKY AND SAND BLOCKS

All the blocks are pieced the same way, but in different color variations. Mix and match the fabrics to make the blocks as scrappy as possible.

1. With right sides together, sew two blue 2½" x 4½" rectangles together as shown. Press the seam allowance as indicated.

Make 13.

2. Sew a blue 2½" x 4½" rectangle to opposite sides of each unit as shown. Press the seam allowances as indicated. Make 13.

Make 13.

3. Sew two blue 2½" x 4½" rectangles together as shown. Press the seam allowance as indicated. Make 26.

Make 26.

4. Sew a unit from step 2 between two units from step 3 as shown. Press the seam allowances as indicated. Make 13 and label them block A.

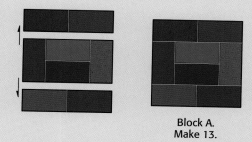

Block A.
Make 13.

5. Repeat steps 1–4 using light brown 2½" x 4½" rectangles. Make seven and label them block B.

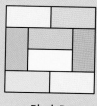

Block B.
Make 7.

6. Repeat steps 1–4 using blue and light brown 2½" x 4½" rectangles to make the required number of blocks in each color arrangement. Label the blocks as shown.

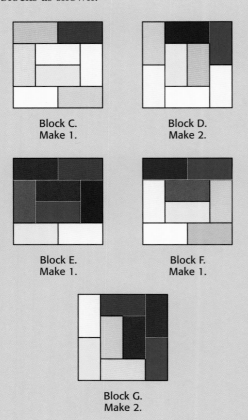

Block C.
Make 1.

Block D.
Make 2.

Block E.
Make 1.

Block F.
Make 1.

Block G.
Make 2.

MAKING THE SMALL STAR BLOCKS

1. Referring to "Triangle Squares" on page 109, use the gold and blue 1⅞" squares to make 56 triangle-square units.

Make 56.

2. Sew two triangle squares together as shown. Press the seam allowance as indicated. Make 28.

Make 28.

3. Sew a gold 2½" square between two units from step 2 as shown. Press the seam allowances as indicated. Make seven.

Make 7.

4. Sew each remaining unit from step 2 between two blue 1½" squares as shown. Press the seam allowances as indicated. Make 14.

Make 14.

5. Sew each unit from step 3 between two units from step 4 as shown. Press the seam allowances as indicated. Make seven.

Make 7.

6. Referring to steps 2–4 of "Making the Sky and Sand Blocks" on page 101, join one unit from step 5 above and six blue 2½" x 4½" rectangles to make a small Star block as shown. Make seven.

Small Star (SS).
Make 7.

MAKING THE LARGE STAR BLOCK

1. Follow steps 1–5 of "Making the Small Star Blocks" on page 102, using four gold and four light gold 1⅞" squares in step 1, and four light gold 1½" squares in step 4, to make one small Star block.

Make 1.

2. Referring to "Triangle Squares" on page 109, use the gold and the blue 2⅞" squares to make eight triangle-square units, each 2½" x 2½".

Make 8.

3. Sew two units from step 2 together as shown. Press the seam allowance as indicated. Make four.

Make 4.

4. Sew the unit from step 1 between two units from step 3 as shown. Press the seam allowances as indicated.

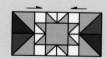

5. Sew each remaining unit from step 3 between two blue 2½" squares as shown. Press the seam allowances as indicated. Make two.

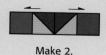

Make 2.

6. Sew the unit from step 4 between the units from step 5 to complete one large Star block as shown. Press the seam allowances as indicated.

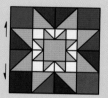

Large Star (LS)

ASSEMBLING THE QUILT TOP

1. Refer to the photo on page 99 and the diagram below. Place blocks A–G and the small and large Star blocks in five rows of seven blocks each, making sure the blocks are oriented as shown. Press the seam allowances in opposite directions from row to row. Sew the rows together; press.

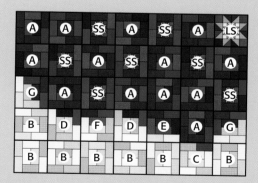

2. Referring to "Borders with Butted Corners" on page 115, sew the light brown 2"-wide strips to the quilt for the inner border. Referring to "Borders with Mitered Corners" on page 116, sew the multicolored 6½" x 60" strips to the sides and the 6½" x 76" strips to the top and bottom of the quilt. Miter the corners.

Quilt assembly

ADDING THE APPLIQUÉS

1. Referring to "Appliqué Basics" on page 111, choose an appliqué method and then use the patterns on pages 105 and 106 to cut out the appliqués from the appropriate fabrics.

2. Working in numerical order, position and appliqué the pieces to the pieced background. Notice that the camels and the second Wise Man overlap the outer border.

3. Use the black and gray embroidery floss and a backstitch or stem stitch to add rope to the camels. Use a black seed bead for each camel's eye.

Backstitch

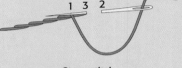

Stem stitch

FINISHING THE QUILT

Refer to "Preparing to Quilt" on page 117, "Quilting Techniques" on page 118, and "Finishing Techniques" on page 119 for more detailed instructions, if needed.

1. Piece the quilt backing so that it is 4" to 6" longer and wider than the quilt top. Mark the quilt top if necessary. Layer the quilt top with batting and backing and baste the layers together—unless you plan to take your quilt to a long-arm quilter.

2. Hand or machine quilt as desired.

3. Trim the batting and backing even with the edges of the quilt top. Add a hanging sleeve if desired. Using the multicolored 2½"-wide strips, prepare the binding and sew it to the quilt.

4. Add additional embellishment to the figures as desired: add leather halters to the camels, beading to decorate the Wise Men, and so on.

5. Make a label and attach it to the back of the quilt.

Appliqué patterns
Enlarge patterns 200%.

Patterns do not include seam allowances.
Reverse patterns for fusible appliqué.

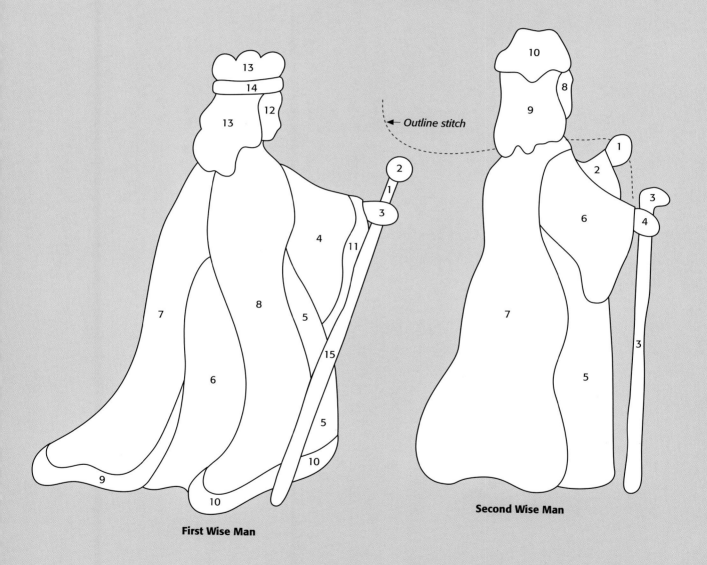

First Wise Man

Second Wise Man

Appliqué patterns

Enlarge patterns 200%.

Patterns do not include seam allowances.
Reverse patterns for fusible appliqué.

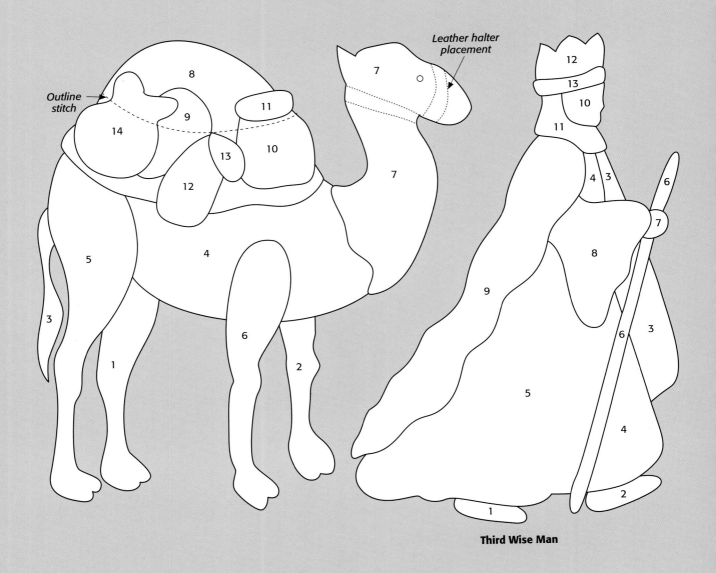

Outline
stitch

Leather halter
placement

Third Wise Man

QUILTMAKING BASICS

Whether you're new to quiltmaking or you're simply ready to learn a new technique, you'll find this quiltmaking basics section filled with helpful information that can make putting your quilt together a pleasurable experience.

FABRICS

Select 100%-cotton fabrics. They hold their shape well and are easy to handle. Cotton blends can be more difficult to stitch and press. Sometimes, however, a cotton blend is worth a little extra effort if it is the perfect fabric for your quilt.

Yardage requirements are provided for all the projects in this book and, unless otherwise noted, are based on 42"-wide fabrics that provide at least 40" of usable fabric after prewashing. Some quilts call for an assortment of scraps or can easily be adapted for a scrappy look. If you have a collection of scraps, feel free to use them and purchase only those fabrics you need to complete the quilt you are making.

SUPPLIES

Sewing machine. To machine piece, you'll need a sewing machine that has a good straight stitch. You'll also need a walking foot or darning foot if you will be doing any machine quilting.

Rotary-cutting tools. You will need a rotary cutter, cutting mat, and acrylic ruler. Rotary-cutting rulers are available in a variety of sizes; some of the most frequently used sizes include 6" x 6", 6" x 24", and 12" x 12" or 15" x 15".

Thread. Use a good-quality, all-purpose cotton or cotton-covered polyester thread.

Needles. For machine piecing, a size 10/70 or 12/80 needle works well for most cottons. For machine quilting, a larger needle, such as a 14/90, works best. For hand appliqué, choose a needle that will glide easily through the edges of the appliqué pieces. Size 10 (fine) to size 12 (very fine) needles work well. For hand quilting, use Betweens, which are short, very sharp needles made specifically for this purpose.

Pins. Long, fine silk pins slip easily through fabric, making them perfect for patchwork. Small sequin pins work well for appliqué, although their shanks are thicker than silk pins.

Scissors. Use your best scissors for cutting fabric only. Use craft scissors to cut paper, fusible web, and template plastic. Sharp embroidery scissors or thread snips are handy for clipping threads.

Template plastic. Use clear or frosted plastic to make durable, accurate templates.

Seam ripper. Use this tool to remove stitches from incorrectly sewn seams.

Marking tools. A variety of tools are available to mark fabric when tracing around templates or marking quilting designs. Use a sharp No. 2 pencil or a fine-lead mechanical pencil on lighter-colored fabrics. Use a silver or chalk pencil on darker fabrics. Chalk pencils or chalk-wheel markers make clear marks on fabric and are easier to remove than grease-based colored pencils. Be sure to test your marking tool to make sure you can remove the marks easily.

ROTARY CUTTING

Instructions for quick and easy rotary cutting are provided wherever possible. All measurements include standard ¼"-wide seam allowances. If you are unfamiliar with rotary cutting, read the steps below.

1. Fold the fabric and match selvages, aligning the crosswise and lengthwise grains as much as possible. Place the folded edge closest to you on the cutting mat. Align a square ruler along the folded edge of the fabric. Place a long, straight ruler to the left of the square ruler, just covering the uneven raw edges of the left side of the fabric.

   Remove the square ruler and cut along the right edge of the long ruler, rolling the rotary cutter away from you. Discard this strip. (Reverse this procedure if you are left-handed.)

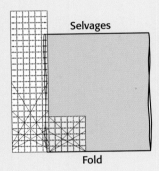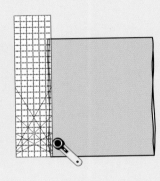

Selvages

Fold

2. To cut strips, align the newly cut edge of the fabric with the ruler markings at the required width. For example, to cut a 3"-wide strip, place the 3" ruler mark on the edge of the fabric.

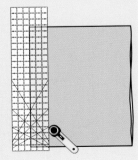

3. To cut squares, cut strips in the required widths. Trim the selvage ends of the strips. Align the left edge of the strips with the correct ruler markings. The sides of the square should have the same measurement as the width of the strips. Cut the strips into squares. Continue cutting squares until you have the number needed.

4. To make a half-square triangle, begin by cutting a square ⅞" larger than the desired finished size of the short side of the triangle. Then cut the square once diagonally, from corner to corner. Each square yields two half-square triangles. The short sides of each triangle are on the straight grain of the fabric.

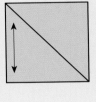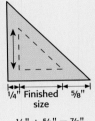

¼" Finished 5/8"
size

¼" + 5/8" = 7/8"

5. To make a quarter-square triangle, begin by cutting a square 1¼" larger than the desired finished size of the long edge of the triangle. Then cut the square twice diagonally, from corner to corner. Each square yields four quarter-square triangles. The long side of each triangle is on the straight grain of the fabric.

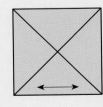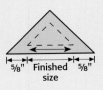

5/8" Finished 5/8"
size

5/8" + 5/8" = 1 ¼"

MACHINE PIECING

Most blocks in this book are designed for easy rotary cutting and quick piecing. Some blocks, however, require the use of templates for particular shapes, such as "Scrappy Circles Baby Quilt" on page 24. Templates for machine piecing include the required ¼"-wide seam allowances. Cut out the templates on the outside lines so that they include the seam allowances. Be sure to mark the pattern name and grain-line arrow on each template.

The most important thing to remember about machine piecing is that you need to maintain a consistent ¼"-wide seam allowance. Otherwise, the quilt blocks won't be the desired finished size. If that happens, the size of everything else in the quilt is affected, including alternate blocks, sashings, and borders. Measurements for all components of each quilt are based on blocks that finish accurately to the desired size plus ¼" on each edge for seam allowances.

Take the time to establish an exact ¼"-wide seam guide on your machine. Some machines have a special presser foot that measures exactly ¼" from the center needle position to the edge of the foot. This feature allows you to use the edge of the presser foot to guide the fabric for a perfect ¼"-wide seam allowance.

If your machine doesn't have such a foot, create a seam guide by placing the edge of a piece of tape or moleskin or a magnetic seam guide ¼" away from the needle.

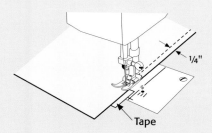
Tape

Chain Piecing

Chain piecing is an efficient system that saves time and thread. It's especially useful when you're making many identical units.

1. Sew the first pair of pieces from cut edge to cut edge, using 12 to 15 stitches per inch. At the end of the seam, stop sewing but don't cut the thread.

2. Feed the next pair of pieces under the presser foot, as close as possible to the first. Continue feeding pieces through the machine without cutting the threads in between the pairs.

3. When all the pieces are sewn, remove the chain from the machine and clip the threads between the pairs of sewn pieces.

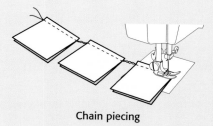
Chain piecing

Triangle Squares

A triangle square is made up of two half-square triangles sewn together. Here is a method of making triangle squares that is fast and accurate.

1. Cut the squares the size specified in the cutting list.

2. Draw a diagonal line from corner to corner on the wrong side of the lighter fabric. Layer two same-sized squares right sides together with the marked square on top and raw edges aligned. Sew ¼" from each side of the drawn diagonal line.

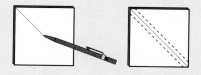

3. Cut on the drawn line. Press the seam allowances toward the darker fabric, unless instructed otherwise, and trim the dog-ears. Each pair of squares will yield two triangle squares.

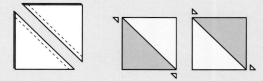

4. Use a square ruler to trim your triangle squares to the correct unfinished size. Place the diagonal line of the ruler on the seam of the triangle square and trim two sides as shown. Rotate the block and trim the other two sides.

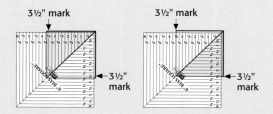

Flying-Geese Units

This is an easy method for constructing four flying-geese units at a time. Each set of four flying geese will be made from one large square and four small squares. The large square will become the triangle in the center of the flying-geese units and the small squares will become the background triangles on each side of the larger triangles.

1. Draw a diagonal line from corner to corner on the wrong side of each small background square.

2. With right sides together, place a background square in opposite corners of a large square, aligning the marked lines as shown. The small squares will overlap slightly in the center of the square. Stitch a scant ¼" from each side of the drawn line.

3. Cut on the marked line to make two separate units. Press the seam allowance toward the background fabric.

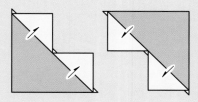

4. With right sides together, place another background square in the corner of each of the two units from step 3 as shown. Stitch a scant ¼" from each side of the marked line.

5. Cut on the marked line of each unit to form two completed flying-geese units. Press the seam allowances toward the background fabric.

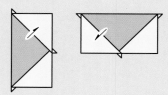

Easing

If two pieces being sewn together are slightly different in size (less than ⅛"), pin the places where the two pieces should match, and in between if necessary, to distribute the excess fabric evenly. Sew the seam with the larger piece on the bottom. The feed dogs will ease the two pieces together.

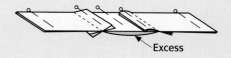

PRESSING

The traditional rule in quiltmaking is to press seam allowances to one side, toward the darker color wherever possible. First press the seams flat from the wrong side of the fabric; then press the seam allowances in the desired direction from the right side. Press carefully to avoid distorting the shapes.

When joining two seamed units, plan ahead and press the seam allowances in opposite directions, as shown. This reduces bulk and makes it easier to match the seams. The seam allowances will butt against each other where two seams meet, making it easier to sew units with perfectly matched seam intersections.

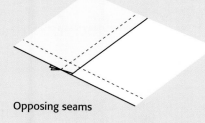

Opposing seams

APPLIQUÉ BASICS

General instructions are provided here for needle-turn, freezer-paper, and fusible appliqué. Even when a specific method of appliqué is mentioned in a project, you are always free to substitute your favorite method. Just be sure to adapt the pattern pieces and project instructions as necessary.

Making Templates

To begin, you will need to make templates of the appliqué patterns. Templates made from clear template plastic are durable and easy to make. Since you can see through the plastic, it is easy to trace the templates accurately from the book page.

Place template plastic over each pattern piece and trace with a fine-line permanent marker. Don't add seam allowances. Cut out the templates on the drawn lines. You need only one template for each different motif or shape. Write the pattern name and mark the grain-line arrow (if applicable) on the template.

Appliquéing by Hand

In traditional hand appliqué, the seam allowances are turned under before the appliqué is stitched to the background fabric. Two traditional methods for turning under the edges are needle-turn appliqué and freezer-paper appliqué. You can use either method to turn under the raw edges, and then use the traditional appliqué stitch to attach the shapes to your background fabric.

Needle-Turn Appliqué

1. Using a plastic template, trace the design onto the right side of the appliqué fabric. Use a No. 2 pencil to mark light fabrics and a white pencil to mark dark fabrics.

2. Cut out the fabric piece, adding a scant ¼"-wide seam allowance all around the marked shape.

3. Position the appliqué piece on the background fabric. Pin or baste in place. If the pieces are numbered, start with piece 1 and add the remaining pieces in numerical order.

4. Starting on a straight edge, use the tip of the needle to gently turn under the seam allowance, about ¼" at a time. Hold the turned seam allowance firmly between the thumb and first finger of one hand as you stitch the appliqué to the background fabric with your other hand. Use a longer needle—a Sharp or milliner's needle—to help control the seam allowance and turn it under neatly. Use the traditional appliqué stitch to sew your appliqué pieces to the background. See "Traditional Appliqué Stitch" on page 112.

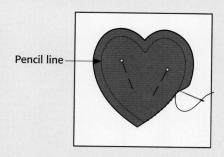

Pencil line

Freezer-Paper Appliqué

Freezer paper, which is coated on one side, is often used to help make perfectly shaped appliqués.

1. Trace around the plastic template on the paper side (not the shiny side) of the freezer paper with a sharp pencil, or place the freezer paper, shiny side down, on top of the pattern and trace.

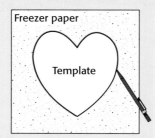

2. Cut out the traced design on the pencil line. Don't add seam allowances.

3. With the shiny side of the paper against the wrong side of your appliqué fabric, iron the freezer-paper cutout in place with a hot, dry iron.

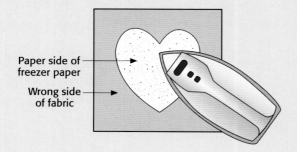

4. Cut out the fabric shape, adding ¼" seam allowances all around the outside edge of the freezer paper.

5. Turn and baste the seam allowance over the freezer-paper edges by hand, or use a fabric glue stick. Clip inside points and fold outside points.

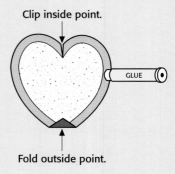

Clip inside point.

GLUE

Fold outside point.

6. Pin or baste the design to the background fabric or block. If the pieces are numbered, start with piece 1 and add the remaining pieces in numerical order. Appliqué the design with the traditional appliqué stitch. See "Traditional Appliqué Stitch" below.

7. Remove any basting stitches. Cut a slit in the background fabric behind the appliqué and remove the freezer paper with tweezers. If you used a glue stick, soak the piece in warm water for a few minutes before removing the freezer paper.

Back of appliqué block

Traditional Appliqué Stitch

The traditional appliqué stitch or blind stitch is appropriate for sewing all appliqué shapes, including sharp points and curves.

1. Thread the needle with a single strand of thread that is approximately 18" long in a color that closely matches the color of your appliqué. Knot the thread tail.

2. Hide the knot by slipping the needle into the seam allowance from the wrong side of the appliqué piece, bringing it out on the fold line.

3. Work from right to left if you are right-handed, or from left to right if you are left-handed. To make the first stitch, insert the needle into the background right next to where the needle came out of the appliqué fabric. Bring the needle up through the edge of the appliqué, about ⅛" from the first stitch.

4. As you bring the needle up, pierce the basted edge of the appliqué piece, catching only one or two threads.

5. Again, take a stitch into the background fabric right next to where the thread came up through the appliqué. Bring the needle up about ⅛" from the previous stitch, again catching the basted edge of the appliqué.

6. Give the thread a slight tug and continue stitching.

   Note that the stitches in the appliqué illustration are drawn large to indicate placement. The stitches should not show in the completed work.

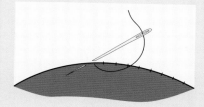

Appliqué stitch

7. To end your stitching, pull the needle through to the wrong side. Behind the appliqué piece, take two small stitches, making knots by taking your needle through the loops.

Fusible Appliqué

Using paper-backed fusible web is a fast and fun way to appliqué. One of the most important things to remember about fusible appliqué is that the appliqué patterns must be the reverse image of the image on the finished project. Appliqué patterns for projects in this book that specify the fusible appliqué method have already been reversed.

Refer to the manufacturer's instructions when applying fusible web to your fabrics; each brand is a little different and pressing it too long may result in fusible web that doesn't stick well.

1. Trace or draw your shape on the paper backing side of the fusible web. Cut out the shape, leaving about a ¼" margin all around the outline.

Fusible web

2. Fuse shapes to the wrong side of your appliqué fabric.

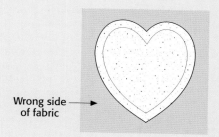

Wrong side of fabric

3. Cut out the shape exactly on the marked line.

4. Remove the paper backing, position the shape on the background fabric, and press it in place with your iron. If the pieces are numbered, start with piece 1 and add the remaining pieces in numerical order.

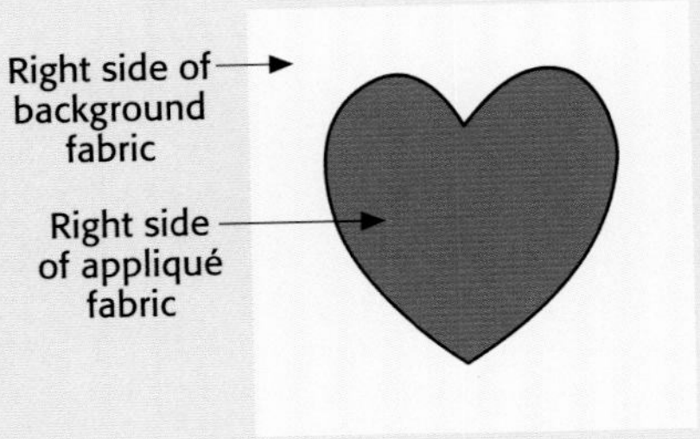

5. If desired, you can add decorative stitches by hand or machine around the edges of the fused appliqués. Commonly used stitches include the satin stitch and blanket stitch.

Making Bias Stems

Bias stems are easy to make with the help of metal or nylon bias press bars. These handy notions are available at most quilt shops and come in sets of assorted widths. The projects in this book use ½" bias bars. The following steps describe the process of making bias stems.

1. Cut the fabric indicated in the materials list for the stems into 1¼"-wide bias strips.

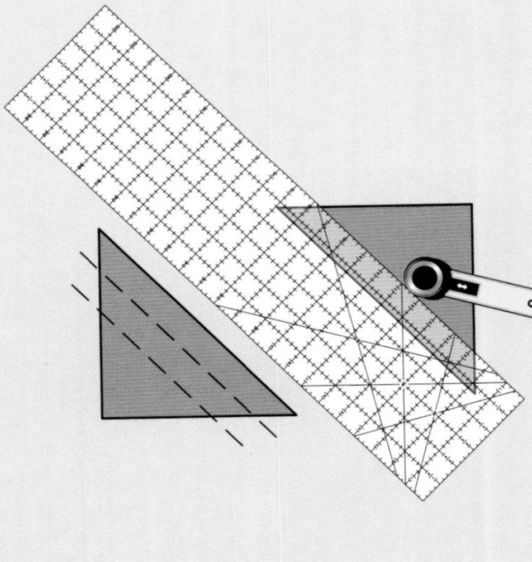

2. Fold each bias strip in half, wrong sides together, and stitch ⅛" from the long raw edges to form a tube.

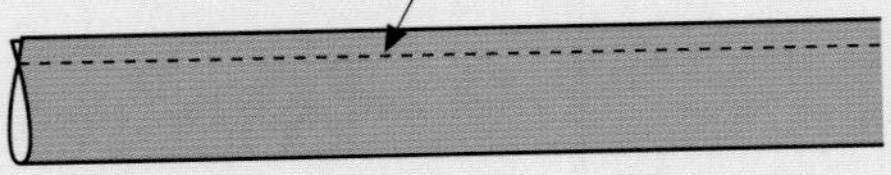

3. Insert the bias bar into the tube, roll the seam to the underside, and press flat. Remove the bias bar.

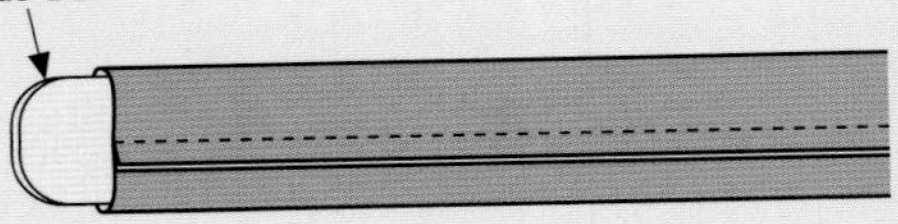

4. Cut the bias tube to the lengths needed and place them on the background fabric as indicated in the project instructions. Pin (or baste) and appliqué the pieces in place.

Squaring Up Blocks

When your blocks are complete, take the time to square them up. Use a large square ruler to measure your blocks and make sure they are the desired size plus an exact ¼" seam allowance on each side. For example, if you are making 9" blocks, they should all measure 9½" before you sew them together. Trim the larger blocks to match the size of the smallest one. Be sure to trim all four sides, or your block will be lopsided.

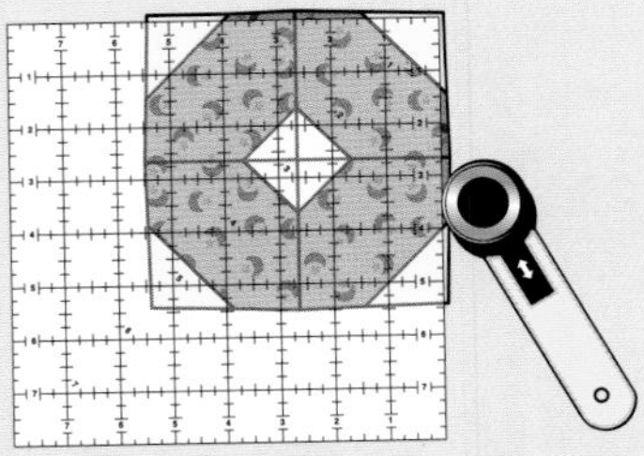

If your blocks aren't the required finished size, adjust all the other components of the quilt, such as sashing and borders, accordingly.

ADDING BORDERS

For best results, don't cut border strips and sew them directly to the quilt without measuring first. The edges of a quilt often measure slightly longer than the distance through the quilt center, due to stretching during construction. Instead, measure the quilt top through the center in both directions to determine how long to cut the border strips. This step ensures that the finished quilt will be as straight and as square as possible, without wavy edges.

Many of the quilts in this book call for plain border strips. These strips generally are cut along the crosswise grain and seamed where extra length is needed. However, some projects call for the borders to be cut on the lengthwise grain so that they don't need to be pieced.

Borders may have butted corners, corner squares, or mitered corners. Check the quilt pattern you are following to see which type of corner treatment you need.

Borders with Butted Corners

1. Measure the length of the quilt top through the center. From the crosswise grain, cut border strips to that measurement, piecing as necessary. Determine the midpoints of the border and quilt top by folding in half and creasing or pinning the centers. Then pin the border strips to opposite sides of the quilt top, matching the center marks and ends and easing as necessary. Sew the border strips in place. Press the seam allowances toward the border strips.

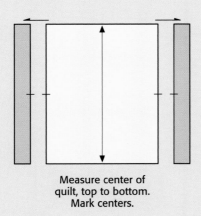

Measure center of
quilt, top to bottom.
Mark centers.

2. Measure the width of the quilt top through the center, including the side border strips just added. From the crosswise grain, cut border strips to that measurement, piecing as necessary. Mark the centers of the quilt edges and the border strips. Pin the border strips to the top and bottom edges of the quilt top, matching the center marks and ends and easing as necessary. Sew the border strips in place. Press the seam allowances toward the border strips.

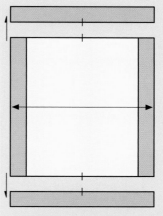

Measure center of quilt, side to
side, including border strips.
Mark centers.

Borders with Corner Squares

1. Measure the width and length of the quilt top through the center.

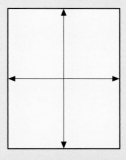

Measure center of quilt top
in both directions.

2. From the crosswise grain, cut border strips to those measurements, piecing as necessary. Mark the centers of the quilt edges and the border strips. Pin the side border strips to opposite sides of the quilt top, matching centers and ends and easing as necessary. Sew the side border strips to the quilt top; press the seam allowances toward the border strips.

3. Cut corner squares of the required size, which is the cut width of the border strips. Sew a corner square to each end of the remaining two border strips; press the seam allowances toward the border strips. Pin the border strips to the top and bottom edges of the quilt top. Match the centers, seams between the border strips and corner squares, and ends. Ease as necessary and stitch. Press the seam allowances toward the border strips.

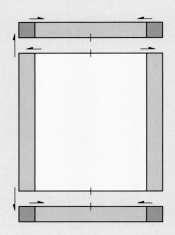

Borders with Mitered Corners

1. Estimate the finished outside dimensions of your quilt, including the border. For example, if your quilt top measures 35½" x 50½" across the center and you want a 5"-wide border, your quilt will measure about 45" x 60" after the border is attached. Add at least ½" to these measurements for seam allowances. To give yourself some leeway, you may want to add an additional 3" to 4" to those measurements. In this example, you would then cut two border strips that measure approximately 48" long and two border strips that measure approximately 63" long.

If your quilt has more than one border, you can sew all the border strips together for each side first and then sew them all to the quilt top at once. When you are mitering the corners, be sure to match the seam intersections of each different border.

2. Fold the quilt in half and mark the centers of the quilt edges. Fold each border strip in half and mark the centers with pins.

3. Measure the length and width of the quilt top across the center. Note the measurements.

4. Place a pin at each end of the side border strips to mark the length of the quilt top. Repeat with the top and bottom border strips.

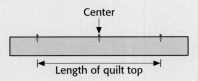

Center

Length of quilt top

5. Pin the border strips to the quilt top, matching the centers. Line up the pins at either end of the border strip with the edges of the quilt. Stitch, beginning and ending ¼" from the raw edges of the quilt top. Repeat with the remaining border strips.

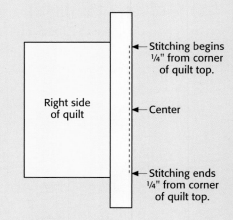

Stitching begins ¼" from corner of quilt top.

Right side of quilt

Center

Stitching ends ¼" from corner of quilt top.

6. Lay the first corner to be mitered on the ironing board. Fold under one border strip at a 45° angle to the other strip. Press and pin.

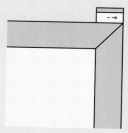

7. Fold the quilt with right sides together, lining up the adjacent edges of the border. If necessary, use a ruler and pencil to draw a line on the crease to make the stitching line more visible. Stitch on the pressed crease, sewing from the previous stitching line to the outside edges.

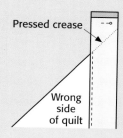

Pressed crease

Wrong side of quilt

8. Press the seam open, check the right side of the quilt to make sure the miters are neat, and then turn the quilt over and trim away the excess border strips, leaving a ¼" seam allowance.

9. Repeat with the remaining corners.

PREPARING TO QUILT

If you'll be quilting your project by hand or on your home sewing machine, you'll want to follow these instructions for marking, layering, basting, and quilting. However, if you plan to have a professional machine quilter quilt your project, check with that person before preparing your finished quilt top in any way. Quilts don't need to be layered and basted for long-arm machine quilting, nor do they usually need to be marked.

Marking the Design

Whether you mark quilting designs on the quilt top or not depends upon the type of quilting you will be doing. Marking is not necessary if you plan to quilt in the ditch (along the seam lines) or outline quilt a uniform distance from seam lines. For more complex quilting designs, however, mark the quilt top before the quilt is layered with batting and backing.

Choose a marking tool that will be visible on your fabric and test it on fabric scraps to be sure the marks can be removed easily. See "Marking tools" on page 107 for options.

Layering and Basting the Quilt

Once you complete the quilt top and mark it for quilting, assemble the quilt "sandwich," which consists of the backing, batting, and the quilt top. The quilt backing and batting should be at least 4" to 6" longer and wider than the quilt top. For large quilts, it is usually necessary to sew two or three lengths of fabric together to make a backing that is large enough. Trim away the selvages before piecing the lengths together. Press the seam allowances open to make quilting easier.

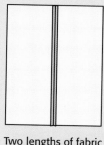

Two lengths of fabric seamed in the center

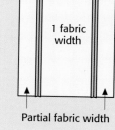

1 fabric width

Partial fabric width

1. Spread the backing wrong side up on a flat, clean surface. Anchor it with pins or masking tape. Be careful not to stretch the backing out of shape.

2. Spread the batting over the backing, smoothing out any wrinkles.

3. Center the pressed quilt top on top of the batting. Smooth out any wrinkles and make sure the quilt-top edges are parallel to the edges of the backing.

4. Starting in the center, baste with needle and thread and work diagonally to each corner. Then baste a grid of horizontal and vertical lines 6" to 8" apart. Finish by basting around the edges.

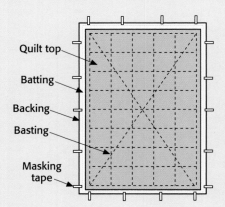

For machine quilting, you can baste the layers with #2 rustproof safety pins. Place pins about 6" to 8" apart, away from the areas you intend to quilt.

QUILTING TECHNIQUES

Some of the projects in this book were hand quilted, others were machine quilted, and some were quilted on long-arm quilting machines. The choice is yours!

Hand Quilting

To quilt by hand, you will need short, sturdy needles (called Betweens), quilting thread, and a thimble to fit the middle finger of your sewing hand. Most quilters also use a frame or hoop to support their work. Use the smallest needle you can comfortably handle; the finer the needle, the smaller your stitches will be. The basics of hand quilting are explained below. For more information on hand quilting, refer to *Loving Stitches: A Guide to Fine Hand Quilting* by Jeana Kimball (Martingale & Company, 2003).

1. Thread your needle with a single strand of quilting thread about 18" long. Make a small knot and insert the needle in the top layer about 1" from the place where you want to start stitching. Pull the needle out at the point where quilting will

begin and gently pull the thread until the knot pops through the fabric and into the batting.

2. Take small, evenly spaced stitches through all three quilt layers. Rock the needle up and down through all layers, until you have three or four stitches on the needle. Place your other hand underneath the quilt so that you can feel the needle point with the tip of your finger when a stitch is taken.

3. To end a line of quilting, make a small knot close to the last stitch. Then backstitch, running the thread a needle's length through the batting. Gently pull the thread until the knot pops into the batting; clip the thread at the quilt's surface.

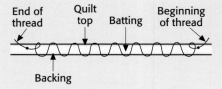

Machine Quilting

Machine quilting is suitable for all types of quilts, from wall hangings to crib quilts to full-size bed quilts. With machine quilting, you can quickly complete quilts that might otherwise languish on the shelves of your sewing room.

For straight-line quilting, a walking foot will help feed the quilt layers through the machine without shifting or puckering. Some machines have a built-in walking foot; others require a separate attachment.

For free-motion quilting, you need a darning foot and the ability to drop or cover the feed dogs on your machine. With free-motion quilting, you guide the fabric in the direction of the design rather than turning the fabric under the needle. Use free-motion quilting to outline quilt a motif or to create stippling or other curved designs.

Professional Quilting

If you prefer to have your quilt quilted by a professional, ask at your local quilt shop for references about someone in your area who does this type of work.

FINISHING TECHNIQUES

Bind your quilt, add a hanging sleeve if one is needed, label your quilt, and you're finished!

Binding

All of the quilts in this book use a French double-fold binding; however, some use straight-cut strips and others use bias strips. If your quilt has curved edges, you must bind your quilt with bias-cut strips; otherwise, straight-cut strips will work fine.

Straight-Cut Binding

Cut strips across the width of the fabric as indicated in the project instructions. Binding strips cut 2½" wide will result in a finished binding that is about ½" wide. (Some quilters prefer narrow binding, especially if a low-loft batting is used.) You will need enough strips to go around the perimeter of the quilt, plus 10" for seams and to turn the corners.

1. Sew the binding strips together to make one long strip. For less bulky seams on the finished binding, overlap the ends of the strips at right angles, right sides together, and stitch across the corner, as shown. Trim the excess fabric and press the seam allowance open. Repeat until all the strips are joined into one long strip.

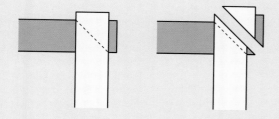

2. Fold the strip in half lengthwise, wrong sides together, and press.

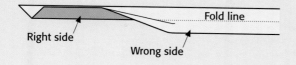

Fold line

Right side

Wrong side

3. Trim the batting and backing even with the quilt top. If you plan to add a hanging sleeve, do so now before attaching the binding (see "Adding a Hanging Sleeve" on page 121).

4. Starting on one side of the quilt and using a ¼"-wide seam allowance, stitch the binding to the quilt, keeping the raw edges even with the quilt-top edge, and leaving a 6" tail unstitched where you start. End the stitching ¼" from the corner of the quilt and backstitch. Clip the threads.

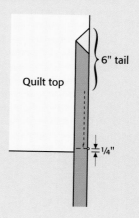

6" tail

Quilt top

¼"

5. Turn the quilt so that you will be stitching down the next side. Fold the binding straight up, away from the quilt, making a 45° angle. Fold the binding back down onto itself, even with the edge of the quilt top. Begin stitching ¼" from the corner, backstitching to secure the stitches. Stitch to the next corner, stopping ¼" from the edge, and repeat the folding and stitching process. Repeat on the remaining edges and corners of the quilt.

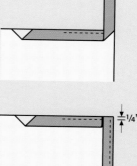

¼"

6. On the last side of the quilt, stop stitching about 7" from where you began. Remove the quilt from the machine. Overlap the ending binding tail with the starting tail. Trim the binding ends with a perpendicular cut so that the overlap is exactly the same distance as the cut width of your binding strips. (If your binding strips are 2½" wide, the overlap should be 2½"; for 2"-wide binding, the overlap should be 2".)

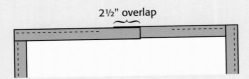
2½" overlap

7. Open up the two ends of the folded binding. Place the tails right sides together so that they join to form a right angle, as shown. Mark a diagonal stitching line from corner to corner and then pin the binding tails together.

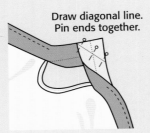
Draw diagonal line.
Pin ends together.

8. Stitch the binding tails together on the marked line. Trim the seam allowance to ¼"; press the seam open to reduce bulk. Refold the binding, align the edges with the raw edges of the quilt top, and finish sewing it in place.

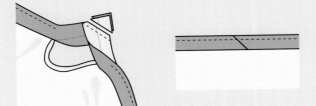

9. Fold the binding over the raw edges to the back of the quilt, with the folded edge covering the row of machine stitching. Hand stitch in place, mitering the corners.

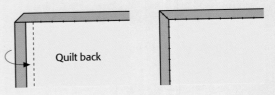
Quilt back

Bias Binding

Consider cutting striped or plaid fabrics on the bias for a dramatic finish.

1. Place a single layer of fabric on your rotary-cutting mat. Using a ruler with a 45°-angle marking, align the 45°-angle line with an edge of the fabric as shown. Cut as many strips as needed to achieve the required length in the width indicated for the project.

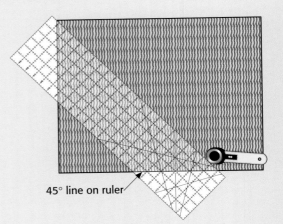
45° line on ruler

2. With right sides together, sew the strips into one long strip, offsetting the seams by ¼" as shown. Press the seam allowances open.

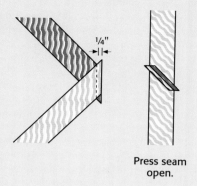

Press seam
open.

3. Follow steps 2–9 of "Straight-Cut Binding" on page 119 to stitch the binding to the quilt edges.

Adding a Hanging Sleeve

If you plan to display your finished quilt on the wall, be sure to add a hanging sleeve to hold the rod.

1. Using leftover fabric from the quilt backing, cut a strip 6" to 8" wide and 1" shorter than the width of your quilt. Fold the ends under ½", and then ½" again to make a hem. Stitch in place.

Fold ends under ½" twice.

2. Fold the fabric strip in half lengthwise, wrong sides together, and baste the raw edges to the top of the quilt back. The top edge of the sleeve will be secured when the binding is sewn on the quilt.

Baste sleeve to top edge of quilt.

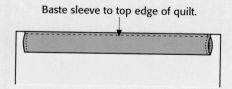

3. Finish the sleeve after the binding has been attached by blindstitching the bottom of the sleeve in place. Push the bottom edge of the sleeve up just a bit to provide a little give; this will keep the hanging rod from putting strain on the quilt.

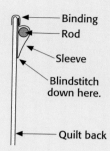

Binding
Rod
Sleeve
Blindstitch
down here.
Quilt back

Signing Your Quilt

Be sure to sign and date your quilt. Future generations will be interested to know more than just who made it and when. Labels can be as elaborate or as simple as you desire. The information can be handwritten, typed, or embroidered. Be sure to include the name of the quilt, your name, your city and state, the date, the name of the recipient if the quilt is a gift, and any other interesting or important information about the quilt.

ABOUT THE CONTRIBUTORS

KARLA ALEXANDER

 Karla has been making quilts in a traditional style for cribs and family beds since she was a young girl. More recently, however, she began exploring the possibilities of quiltmaking and developing her own style and methods. Today she self-publishes a diverse line of quilt patterns through her company, Saginaw Street Quilt Company. And she is the author of books, including *Stack the Deck!* (Martingale & Company, 2002) and her most recent publication, *New Cuts for New Quilts* (2006), also published by Martingale & Company.

A significant part of Karla's life is spent teaching others to embrace the world of quiltmaking. Her books and teaching style encourage visual play—endless variations of arrangements without preconceived notions of the end result. She sees her designs simply as the starting point for another quiltmaker's inspiration.

MAAIKE BAKKER

 Maaike, who is from the Netherlands, made her first quilt in 1978 as a wedding gift for friends. In 1993, during a trip to the United States, she became enthusiastic about foundation piecing. She published her first quilting book in Dutch and has also published a book in German. Maaike has written three books with Martingale & Company, including *Strip-Pieced Quilts* (2005) and *Spellbinding Quilts* (2006).

Today Maaike lives and works in a little village in the north of the Netherlands. She designs her quilts and writes books and articles in her old farmhouse studio. She also teaches patchwork techniques, and her quilts have been exhibited in the Netherlands, Germany, and the United States. Maaike and her husband, Theo, have three children.

RACHEL W. N. BROWN

Rachel learned to sew at an early age at her mother's Singer sewing machine set up in the kitchen. But it wasn't until she moved to Franklin County, Virginia, in 1972 with her pastor husband that she was introduced to serious quiltmaking. Rachel's first quilt was made by measuring fabric strips with a yardstick and cutting patches with scissors. Although that quilt turned out to be 1" wider at the top than at the bottom, it remains one of her favorites.

These days Rachel is busy sewing, designing, and managing things at her shop, Rachel's Quilt Patch, which is housed in the historic train station in Staunton, Virginia. She and her husband, Dennis, reside in Mount Sidney with their miniature schnauzer and two rescued cats.

TERRY BURKHART AND ROZAN MEACHAM

Terry is the former owner of the quilt shop Pieceable Dry Goods in Kennewick, Washington, and Rozan has been a popular teacher at the shop. They share a love of collecting antiques and displaying and using their treasures in their homes. Their passion for antique quilts and other forms of American folk art are evident in their book, *Primitive Gatherings* (Martingale & Company, 2006). Rozan, motivated by respect for the women who walked before her, pays tribute to the past through her own unique folk-art designs. And Terry enjoys a connection to history every day. She lives in an 1899 farmhouse on her husband's family wheat farm, which has been an inspiration for many of her stitchery and quilt designs.

CORI DERKSEN AND MYRA HARDER

Cori and Myra are business partners from Winkler, Manitoba, Canada. Their project featured in this book is from *The Blessed Home Quilt,* their fifth book published by Martingale & Company. Through their company, Blue Meadow Designs, they design and wholesale quilt patterns and have recently begun designing fabrics for RJR Fabrics. They also teach, present trunk shows, and host an annual event called Hometown Retreat.

These two young mothers each have a son and a daughter, and they spend the long Canadian winters quilting. Cori also enjoys expressing her talents through gardening and scrapbooking, while Myra likes to draw, design quilts, read, and spend time in the summer at the lake with her family.

KIM DIEHL

As a young girl, Kim slept under her grandmother's hand-pieced quilts, but it wasn't until 1998 that she discovered quiltmaking for herself. From her very first quilt, Kim felt the urge to redesign elements of the project so that it would reflect her own tastes and personal style. She finds that as she creates each new quilt, her love of the design process continues to grow and flourish.

After winning *American Patchwork and Quilting* magazine's "Pieces of the Past" quilt challenge in 1998, Kim began designing quilts professionally and has seen her work published in several national magazines. While Kim continues to design projects for *American Patchwork and Quilting,* she is currently at work on her third book with Martingale & Company. Kim and her family make their home in Idaho, where they enjoy the clear blue skies and simple lifestyle that living in the Northwest brings.

SUSAN TEEGARDEN DISSMORE

Susan began quilting in 1994 after opening her fabric shop. She soon began to design her own quilts for exclusive use at the shop. Though she recently closed her store, she continues to quilt and is the author of several quilt books with Martingale & Company, including *Better by the Dozen* (2006) and *Clever Quarters* (2004). She delights in the design process and loves to incorporate scraps into her quilt projects. Susan and her husband, Tim, have two sons, Blake and Justin. She and her family reside in Federal Way, Washington.

ANN FRISCHKORN AND AMY SANDRIN

Ann and Amy are quiltmaking partners—and identical twin sisters—who live more than 2,000 miles apart. Ann lives outside of Chicago and Amy lives near Seattle. Their quiltmaking journey began when Ann took a beginner's quilting class and knew after the first stitch that this was an art form she would embrace for the rest of her life. Not one to miss out, Amy decided to give quilting a try too. They have been avidly quilting since 1992.

These sisters have published three quilting books, the most recent being *Scraps of Time: Quilting with Treasured Fabrics* (Martingale & Company, 2006). They have also appeared on HGTV's *Simply Quilts,* hosted by Alex Anderson. In their spare time, Ann and Amy collaborate on novels.

JUDY HOPKINS

Judy comes from a family of quilters: her grandmother, her mother, and her aunt all made quilts. She started pursuing a full-time career in quilting after being named Alaska's state winner of the Great American Quilt Contest in 1986.

Judy has authored 15 design and pattern books for quilters, including the three-volume *Around the Block* series and *101 Fabulous Rotary-Cut Quilts* (with Nancy J. Martin). Her love of scrap-bag quilts, old and new, led to the design of her popular Scrap-Master ruler, a tool for quick-cutting half-square triangles from irregularly shaped scraps.

Judy lives in Juneau, Alaska, with her husband, Bill. And she has five grandchildren who like to help her sew.

LORAINE MANWARING AND SUSAN NELSEN

Loraine and Susan are sisters and coauthors of *All Buttoned Up,* (Martingale & Company, 2006). Loraine started sewing at the age of eight when she was given a small Singer sewing machine. Her grandmother helped her sew a dress for herself on the tiny chain-stitch machine, and she has loved sewing ever since. When her children were young, she taught basic sewing to a women's group at church, and this led to teaching quilting classes as well. She has been teaching various fabric arts ever since and has been designing her own patterns and quilting projects for years.

Susan loves the creative experience of working with fabrics and colors, and she thrives on designing quilts for her original quilt-pattern company, Rasmatazz Designs. Susan also operates a long-arm machine-quilting business.

Loraine and her husband, Mark, raised their family in Washington State and currently live in Utah at the foot of the rugged Wasatch Mountains. Susan and her husband, Ken, moved to Idaho Falls, Idaho, following Ken's retirement.

NANCY J. MARTIN

Nancy is a talented teacher and quiltmaker who has written more than 40 books on quiltmaking. An innovator in the quilting industry, she introduced the Bias Square cutting ruler to quilters everywhere. Nancy was the 2002 recipient of the prestigious Silver Star Award, presented by Quilts, Inc., the sponsor of the largest biannual trade show in the quilting industry—International Quilt Market and Festival.

Along with having more than 25 years of teaching experience and several bestselling titles to her credit, Nancy is the founder of Martingale & Company, the publisher of America's Best-Loved Quilt Books®. She and her husband, Dan, enjoy living in the Pacific Northwest.

TERRY MARTIN

Terry is the author of five quilting books, and *Variations on a Theme: Quilts with Easy Options* (Martingale & Company, 2006) is her most recent. She loves to lecture and teach quilting classes. She is a member of her local guild, Busy Bee Quilt Guild of Snohomish, Washington, and she is always willing to head off for a weekend of quilting at a local retreat. She enjoys the friendship, support, and never-ending laughter that her quilting friends provide her. Terry, her husband, and college-aged daughter live in western Washington.

ANNE MOSCICKI

Anne is the owner of Touchwood Quilt Design, a company created for quilters just like herself—busy women who place high value on their families and time, and enjoy creating projects that reflect that personal style. Anne's childhood interests in art and crafts led her to combine a love of quilting with her award-winning career as an art director for print media. In addition to authoring *Time to Quilt* and *Joined at the Heart* (with Linda Wyckoff-Hickey), Anne has created patterns that have been featured in national quilting magazines. She lives with her husband, two daughters, and a spoiled-rotten West Highland terrier in Lake Oswego, Oregon.

CLAUDIA OLSON

Claudia has been quilting for about 20 years. After taking a class from Marsha McCloskey, she was inspired to look at quilt blocks and patterns in a new way to create her own unique designs. Since then, no quilt pattern has been safe from tweaking! Claudia likes to experiment with block combinations and looks for ways to make secondary patterns stand out.

This native Californian now resides in eastern Washington State. She is the author of several quilt books, including *Two-Block Appliqué Quilts* (Martingale & Company, 2004) and *Two-Block Theme Quilts* (Martingale & Company, 2006). Claudia enjoys teaching quilt classes, writing, designing new quilts, and traveling.

JANNA L. SHEPPARD

Janna, the author of *Courtship Quilts,* was born and raised in the nation's Sweetheart City, Loveland, Colorado. She graduated from the University of Northern Colorado with a degree in vocational home economics and taught home economics classes in Nevada from 1989 to 1997. Now retired from teaching, Janna enjoys quilting full time.

JULIA TETERS-ZIEGLER

Julia was an art major in college, where she met the love of her life, married, and started her family. She enjoyed smocking when her children were babies, and continues to dabble in knitting, painting, and scrapbooking. But her true passion has always been quilting.

Julia currently works at the Quilted Dragon in Lakewood, Washington. She teaches and has a small pattern business. She is a member of the Association of Pacific Northwest Quilters, a charter member of the Washington Stars Quilt Guild, a member of the Comforters Quilt Guild, and a charter member of Quilters by the Bay.

With children grown, Julia and her husband, Jack, are empty nesters in Olympia, Washington. You can learn more at Julia's Web site, www.just-julia.com.

CATHY WIERZBICKI

Although she has been a dedicated quilter since the mid-1990s, quilting is just one of many interests that Cathy Wierzbicki enjoys. The list of her wide-ranging interests is long and includes all sorts of crafting, needlework, and more. Her favorite pastime of all is spending time at a Minnesota lake with her husband, Tom, their two grown children, and one very special grandson.

Cathy currently makes her home in the Pacific Northwest. She has three other books to her credit, including *Coffee-Time Quilts: Super Projects, Sweet Recipes* (Martingale & Company, 2004), and she is the creator of the All-In-One Ruler™. *Twosey-Foursey Quilts* (2006) is her second book with Martingale & Company.

New and Bestselling Titles from

America's Best-Loved Craft & Hobby Books®
America's Best-Loved Knitting Books®

America's Best-Loved Quilt Books®

APPLIQUÉ
Adoration Quilts
Appliqué at Play *NEW!*
Appliqué Takes Wing
Easy Appliqué Samplers
Favorite Quilts
    from Anka's Treasures *NEW!*
Garden Party
Mimi Dietrich's Baltimore Basics *NEW!*
Raise the Roof
Stitch and Split Appliqué
Tea in the Garden

FOCUS ON WOOL
Hooked on Wool
Purely Primitive
Simply Primitive
Warm Up to Wool

GENERAL QUILTMAKING
All Buttoned Up *NEW!*
Alphabet Soup
American Doll Quilts
Calendar Kids *NEW!*
Cottage-Style Quilts
Creating Your Perfect Quilting Space
Creative Quilt Collection Volume One
Dazzling Quilts *NEW!*
Follow the Dots . . . to Dazzling Quilts
Follow-the-Line Quilting Designs
Follow-the-Line Quilting Designs
    Volume Two
Fresh Look at Seasonal Quilts, A *NEW!*
Merry Christmas Quilts
Prairie Children and Their Quilts *NEW!*
Primitive Gatherings
Quilt Revival
Sensational Sashiko
Simple Traditions

LEARNING TO QUILT
Blessed Home Quilt, The
Happy Endings, Revised Edition
Let's Quilt!
Magic of Quiltmaking, The
Quilter's Quick Reference Guide, The
Your First Quilt Book (or it should be!)

PAPER PIECING
40 Bright and Bold Paper-Pieced Blocks
300 Paper-Pieced Quilt Blocks
Easy Machine Paper Piecing
Quilt Block Bonanza
Quilter's Ark, A
Show Me How to Paper Piece
Spellbinding Quilts *NEW!*

PIECING
40 Fabulous Quick-Cut Quilts
101 Fabulous Rotary-Cut Quilts
365 Quilt Blocks a Year: Perpetual Calendar
1000 Great Quilt Blocks
Better by the Dozen
Big 'n Easy
Border Workbook, 10th Anniversary
    Edition, The *NEW!*
Clever Quarters, Too *NEW!*
Lickety-Split Quilts
New Cuts for New Quilts *NEW!*
Over Easy
Sew One and You're Done
Simple Chenille Quilts
Snowball Quilts *NEW!*
Stack a New Deck
Sudoku Quilts *NEW!*
Two-Block Theme Quilts
Twosey-Foursey Quilts *NEW!*
Variations on a Theme
Wheel of Mystery Quilts

QUILTS FOR BABIES & CHILDREN
Even More Quilts for Baby
More Quilts for Baby
Quilts for Baby
Sweet and Simple Baby Quilts

SCRAP QUILTS
More Nickel Quilts
Nickel Quilts
Save the Scraps
Scraps of Time
Simple Strategies for Scrap Quilts *NEW!*
Successful Scrap Quilts from
    Simple Rectangles
Treasury of Scrap Quilts, A

CRAFTS
Bag Boutique
Greeting Cards Using Digital Photos
It's a Wrap
Miniature Punchneedle Embroidery
Passion for Punchneedle, A *NEW!*
Scrapbooking Off the Page…and on
    the Wall

KNITTING & CROCHET
365 Knitting Stitches a Year:
    Perpetual Calendar
Crochet from the Heart
Cute Crochet for Kids *NEW!*
First Crochet
First Knits
Fun and Funky Crochet
Funky Chunky Knitted Accessories
Handknit Style II *NEW!*
Knits from the Heart
Knits, Knots, Buttons, and Bows
Knitter's Book of Finishing Techniques, The
Little Box of Crocheted Hats and Scarves,
    The
Little Box of Knitted Throws, The
Little Box of Scarves, The
Modern Classics *NEW!*
Pursenalities
Saturday Sweaters
Sensational Knitted Socks
Silk Knits *NEW!*
Yarn Stash Workbook, The